GOOD PRACTICE IN EQUAL OPPORTUNITIES

Good Practice in Equal Opportunities

ROSE GILROY
University of Newcastle upon Tyne

With a contribution by SIMON MARVIN

Avebury

Aldershot · Brookfield USA · Hong Kong · Singapore · Sydney

Published by
Avebury
Ashgate Publishing Group
Gower House
Croft Road
Aldershot
Hants. GU11 3HR
England

Ashgate Publishing Company
Old Post Road
Brookfield
Vermont, 05036
USA

A CIP catalogue record for this book is available from the British Library.

ISBN 1 85628 334 8

Printed and Bound in Great Britain by
Athenaeum Press Ltd., Newcastle upon Tyne.

Contents

Acknowledgments

My debts of gratitude are so many that undoubtedly I will fail in the attempt to be all embracing. My thanks to the following:

Barbara McLoughlin of Manchester City Council for the "Pedestrian Subways and Personal Safety report and the "Planning a Safer Environment for Women" prepared by the Planning for Women group.

Wendy Barber, Claire Mitcham, Franklin Riley and Lucy Wilkinson for permission to quote from their dissertations and option studies.

The Institute of Housing whose working group on equal opportunities gave rise to the employment chapter.

The Local Government Management Board for inspiration prompted by their excellent video 'The Disabling Council'.

Simon Marvin for his contribution on utilities and for sorting out all the technical side of production.

All my students whose discussions have stimulated me to further thought.

Rose Gilroy
Newcastle University
September 1992

Abbreviations

ACR	Association for Consumer Research
APTC	Ancilliary, Professional, Technical & Clerical
BSI	British Standards Institute
BT	British Telecom
CRE	Commission for Racial Equality
CSDP	Chronically Sick and Disabled Persons Act
DoE	Department of the Environment
DSS	Department of Social Security
EOC	Equal Opportunities Commission
HAG	Housing Association Grant
LBC	London Borough Council
LGTB	Local Government Training Board
MBC	Metropolitan Borough Council
NACAB	National Association of Citizens' Advice Bureaux
NCC	National Consumer Council
NFHA	National Federation of Housing Associations
OFFER	Office of Electricity Regulation
OFGAS	Office of Gas Supply
OFTEL	Office of Telecommunications
OFWAT	Office of Water Supply
OPCS	Office of Population and Census Survey
PAN	Planning Advice Note
PATH	Positive Action Training in Housing
PPG	Planning Practice Guidelines
PUAF	Public Utilities Access Forum
RNIB	Royal National Institute for the Blind
RNID	Royal National Institute for the Deaf
RRB	Race Relations Board

RTPI	Royal Town Planning Institute
TUC	Trade Union Congress
UDP	Unitary Development Plan
UPIAS	Union of Physically Impaired Against Segregation
WHO	World Health Organisation

Foreword

No quality without equality

It may seem odd, perhaps out dated, to be talking of equal opportunities issues. This was the buzz word of the 1980s when local authorities, in particular, began to examine the anti discrimination legislation of the seventies and carve out good practice models to help them fulfil their legal duties under the two acts: The Race Relations Act 1976 and The Sex Discrimination Act 1975. Their examination of policy and practice to eradicate unnecessary and artificial barriers led to many radical stances particularly in the field of employment. There was also a recognition of the importance of staff training to root out discriminatory views that could so easily be institutionalised into practices and into policies which rendered certain groups second class citizens or even invisible.

When we think of those services which were in the forefront of fighting discrimination it is Education and Personnel (recruitment and training) which are uppermost in our minds with Housing trailing in third following the investigations of the CRE which revealed racism in public sector allocation, mortgage lending, estate agency practice and accommodation bureaux. Planning is not among this number though a small number of local planning authorities, namely Leicester City Council, Sheffield City Council and some of the London Boroughs were instrumental in raising a new agenda for the profession.

These were the concerns of the eighties so why worry about these issues now? The 'e' has been dropped and there is a new buzz word: 'quality'. At every turn there are mini citizens charters and customer charters setting out standards of service and channels for complaint and redress. In Local Government the phrases 'total quality management' and 'quality standards'

ix

are on everyone's lips while the pursuit of BS 5750 has become the new Holy Grail. If this is to be a meaningful philosophy not another trend then considerable culture change needs to be made within organisations. The setting up and delivery of a quality service means **valuing** members of the public as **customers** and **citizens**. This new thinking can only lead us back to equality since the **whole** community can be viewed as customers and citizens. Furthermore it means that in order to produce plans that will meet the needs of these customers, the policy makers need to understand those needs. It may be that many of those who plan or carry out the implementation have little comprehension how the policies and practices affect groups whose lifestyles, whose needs, whose difficulties are very different from their own. This raises issues about staff training to increase sensitivity as well as employment issues about how staff should mirror the client group that is both black and white, both male and female, both able bodied and disabled, young people and older people.

This book sets out to reassert the importance of equality in the pursuit of quality services for all.

The current climate

To attempt to summarise the position on equal opportunities issues is to look at a confused picture. Having passed legislation in the seventies on both gender and race, there seems little likelihood of further legislation from central government. In 1991 John Major launched Operation 2000 with the aim of stimulating the business world to recognise the unlocked potential of women workers and thus to set equal opportunities targets. This strategy was launched against a background of a very poor level of child care provision and the rejection of tax concessions on child care costs for working mothers.

On the issue of race, central government remains ambivalent with no new powers for the CRE though government has accepted new codes of practice in public and private sector housing which give more guidance to those looking for models. None of these codes are mandatory, indicating that far from proceeding to a new regulatory era, the ethos is still one of voluntarism. Prior to the general election in 1991, there was parliamentary discussion of proposals to tighten the law regarding the entry of refugees and those wishing to claim asylum. While this was overtaken by the election, it seems that this is not a dead issue but one which will resurface in due course no doubt adding fuel to the arguments that British immigration legislation is based on racism.

In the area of disability another attempt, a private members bill introduced by Alf Roberts MP, to create anti discrimination legislation was defeated. Mounting pressure from MPs and the growing vocal pressure groups of disabled people surely must result in change before long. This may be the triumph of hope over experience: is government likely to give money to the setting up of another watch-dog body and, more fundamentally, given Mrs Thatcher's assertion that there is no such thing as society is this government likely to introduce legislation which recognises the operation of discrimination against a particular group by society?

Heterosexism remains perplexing. As the law stands lesbians and their relationships are invisible while gay men must be consenting, over twenty one and must confine their sexual activity to behind closed and private doors. Just prior to the 1991 election John Major was known to have had talks with Sir Ian McKellen, a well known campaigner for gay rights, which may mean that government is contemplating change, a view reinforced by the positive speeches made by Edwina Currie in support of lowering the age of consent. Creating a tension is the Local Government Act 1988, clause 28 inserted into the Local Government Act 1986 (Section 2A), which forbids local authorities from promoting homosexuality or teaching that homosexuality is an acceptable family relationship. The law does not forbid the challenging of discrimination against gay men and lesbians in equal opportunities policies though the existence of clause 28 may well have caused the censorship of anti discriminatory actions and the belief that discrimination can be ignored or even encouraged.

A confused picture with some issues of discrimination receiving legislative backing for what that is worth (race and gender); some still subject to discriminatory laws (gay men) and some dismissed as being matters of physical access not discrimination on a broader front (disability). Age is nowhere on this agenda: it remains the unrecognised discrimination.

However mixed the messages from central government, with the promotion of a quality service in mind, there is an imperative on those in public services of all kinds to eradicate discrimination and to promote equality of opportunity.

But what is equality of opportunity?

For some authorities, as numerous pieces of research has proven, equality of opportunity is simply not acting in a blatantly discriminatory fashion. This is one aspect but not the whole story. The Race Relations Act 1976 lays a duty on local authorities to promote equality of opportunity and good race relations. If this duty is taken by public bodies as impetus to take action on a whole range of discriminations then we need to see action not an absence of action. Action usually falls into the regulatory category that is the reform of procedures and elimination of discriminatory barriers or into the redistributive category which opens up the service to previously excluded groups or targets resources upon their needs.

The usual beginning is to formulate an equal opportunities policy. In some quarters this action is both an end and a beginning leading to the belief that equal opportunities policies have all the ring of sincerity associated with the health warnings on cigarette packets. It is vital that action follows the policy if it is not to be seen as a token gesture or posturing by an organisation which is zealous of its image but unwilling to undergo the painful process of change.

The following is an extract from Orbit Housing Association 's equal opportunity statement which typically embraces a range of activities with the emphasis on the regulatory (eradicating discriminatory practice) but with some claims to looking at redistribution.

In supporting the National Federation of Housing Association's policy Orbit Housing Association is mindful of the commitment in all its areas of operation and therefore can confirm that:
1. In the provision of housing services, and employment of staff to provide these services, the Association seeks to ensure equality of opportunity and treatment for all persons.
2. No person or group of persons applying for housing, or for a job, or for contracts or work with the Association, is treated less favourably than any other person or group of persons because of their race, colour, ethnic or national origin or because of their religion, sex or physical disability.
3. In carrying out this policy the Association assists minority groups to benefit equally from its housing services and to identify their needs within its area of operation. For this reason applicants for housing or employment are invited to help the Association to maintain and monitor its records by indicating on the forms provided, their ethnic origin.
4. Where genuine occupational reasons exist, the Association expects to employ staff from minority groups and if necessary to provide them appropriate opportunities to enable them to compete or qualify for positions in the Association's staff structure.

Other policies might include a clause setting out the organisation's attitude to harassment or discriminatory acts carried out by staff:

A policy statement is important in defining the scope and aim of action aim, acting as a focus for change and a clear signal to staff and customers of the service that there is a mood of change. But every organisation needs to consider that:

• A policy is not a substitute for action and it is important that an early beginning is made of an audit of policy, practice, language and attitudes with a view to introducing a timetabled programme of change.

• Before good practice can be introduced it must be identified, which can be done by looking at the examples set by other organisations, talking to advice agencies and other campaigning bodies and more importantly getting into discussion with user groups in the area. What do they think about the service, what ideas do they have for change?

• The audit should lead to the setting of targets in terms of changing individuals (training programme and targets for recruitment) and changing the organisation (timetables for changing procedures).

• Change needs to be monitored.

• Positive images of service users and providers can be provided through posters, careful use of images in explanatory leaflets and promotional material.

These action points are common to organisations seeking to implement equal opportunities but concentrating on instituting non discriminatory procedures. An organisation dedicated to redistributive action might consider the following positive uses of policy:

• Giving grants to new or existing black businesses through schemes such as the Sheffield Ethnic Minority Business Initiative which is a city council scheme helping black business start up (Sheffield City Council, 1991).

• Targeting housing finance such as Estate Action and supplementary allocations for Renewal Areas on areas where there is a concentration of black citizens with poor living conditions.

• Targeting programmes such as City Challenge on black areas to make an all-round investment in housing, schools, shopping areas, leisure facilities, small businesses.

• Setting targets for the recruitment of members from minority groups onto housing association committees or as advisers to committees.

• Identifying land for the building of a mosque or sheltered housing for black elders.

• Grant aiding bodies which represent the views of minority groups.

• Using the enabling role to promote the meeting of housing, leisure, employment and other needs by external bodies.

These are a few examples but each organisation must decide what its aims are in respect of equal opportunities - will it stop at regulating its practices and procedures or does it aim to take positive action to reduce inequalities.

About this book

This book was borne out of the experience of teaching equal opportunities issues to undergraduate planning students. This course set out to challenge the proposition that:

In town planning education, students go through four years full time study and in this period they are fed an educational diet of implicit and explicit racist and sexist assumptions (Grey and Amooquaye, 1990).

In this course we attempted to assert that while planning and plan making is about using land and buildings it is about considering how their use can benefit the people who live and work in an area.

The opening section of the book examines areas of discrimination: racism, sexism including heterosexism, ageism and discrimination against the disabled. The aim of this section is to raise awareness of:

• the fact that minority groups experience greater social and economic deprivation than white, middle class, heterosexual, able bodied, non-elderly men.

• the extent to which this deprivation is due to discrimination which denies them equality of rights and opportunities.

• the way in which discrimination operates in both overt and covert fashion.

• the way discrimination results from a fusion of individual attitudes and institutional responses in the form of practice and policy.

In no way does this cover every aspect of discrimination nor, indeed every discrimination. There is no discussion of class though it is plain that women, black men and women, disabled people and the elderly all escape some (but certainly not all) of the 'slings and arrows' if they are middle class, professional and better off.

The second section relates these areas of discrimination to specific policy areas: planning for people; planning for multi-racial Britain; planning for safety and access; housing; access to utility services focusing on water, energy and telecommunications; and, finally work and employment. Each chapter examines a range of common problems and suggests ways of working whereby the service fits around the customers needs rather than setting up a Procrustean bed which is the way many services operate. The tone is practical though reference is made to a large body of views both practitioner and academic.

It is hoped that this book will provide food for thought and give practitioners, teachers and students the impetus, perhaps the courage, to put people back at the centre of their practice. It does not suggest that the old blue prints are thrown away and these new ones put in their place; if anything it asserts that there are no blueprints only perhaps a few golden rules:

• listen don't talk.

• places belong to the people not professionals be they housing officers, planners or whoever.

• practice what you preach.

References

Grey, G. and Amooquaye, E. (1990), "A New Agenda for Race and Planning" in Montgomery, J. and Thornley, A. (eds), *Radical Planning Initiatives*, Gower, London.

Sheffield City Council (1991), The Draft Unitary Development Plan.

Section 1
Discrimination

Chapter 1

Racism

"I can't!"
"Go on, it'll be a laugh!"
Shelley fixed it all up. He's her brother's friend, older, blond and
gorgeous too.
We scribbled each other a couple of notes beforehand. Amazing, another
Prince fan! Vegetarian too!
Eventually the big day comes. I end up wearing my black dress.
Catching my reflection in a shop window - not bad! Shelley's done a
good job on the hair. Hope he's not too late, it'll get windswept.
"There he is," she nudges me, and points. He looks at me strangely (I
told her I put too much make-up on).
"It's a bloody Paki"
(Selvarajah, 1992)

Refugee Housing Association has been found guilty of discrimination
against Afro-Caribbean clients following investigation by the
Commission for Racial Equality. The CRE was first alerted in January
1990 by a worker from a resettlement project alleging that Refugee's St
Francis House hostel in Bristol had turned away Afro-Caribbean people
because of objections from other tenants (Inside Housing, 1992).

In their 1990 Annual Report the Commission for Racial Equality stated

the pervasiveness and deep rootedness of racism requires us to be
continually vigilant and to understand that, simply because it no longer
finds the same expression, it has not been erased (CRE, 1990:7).

In 1988 the television series featuring two actors, one black and one
white, revealed repeated rejection on the grounds of skin colour. There were

no notices saying 'No coloureds' as there might have been 30 years ago; such declarations are now unlawful but the effect was the same. It has been pointed out that the real impact of anti discrimination legislation has been to convert the white born British into a nation of hypocrites. There is a growing black middle class but here, as in the United States, the ability of some groups or individuals to get on does not suggest that basic inequalities have been addressed, much less eradicated. At the present moment the results of the 1991 census are awaited eagerly by social scientists as a quarry for research. What might this census reveal about the black population in Britain? Will we echo Colin Brown's depressing statement that 'Britain's well established black population is still occupying the precarious and unattractive position of the earlier immigrants'?

A survey undertaken in the early part of 1992 in Newcastle as part of City Challenge base line monitoring revealed racism distorting the lives of children and adults

The colour of our skin will stop us getting a job (Class 8, Rutherford School)

Unemployment in the ethnic minority community is much higher. We want our youngsters to be given a chance. Those born in this country they are educated in this country, they have degrees, they have the qualifications. But they are working in the restaurants, washing the dishes, they are working in shops (Newcastle University, 1992: 77).

In the past it has been easier, perhaps, to camouflage racism or lack of race awareness in publicly delivered services by hiding behind the barrier of language. It was easier to stereotype black people as immigrants whose inability to speak English was a problem and the primary reason for poor access to services (Ratcliffe, 1992: 393). This explains the high emphasis placed upon translation of documentation and the availability of translators. Language cannot be ignored as an issue: all organisations need to consider how well equipped they are to overcome language barriers by using translation and interpretation facilities and the employment of bilingual staff as well as examining the attitudes of staff to customers who don't have good command of English. Nevertheless, access to information is only one facet of the issue. While information can be seen as a source of power in a pluralistic political system and as a means of helping the under-represented participate more effectively, it does not begin to address the historical or structural character of inequality. If language had been the only problem Caribbeans would have enjoyed the same access to quality services given to whites!

Language is now becoming a secondary issue as, increasingly, the black population is a population born in these islands with English as a first or equal language.

No black in the Union Jack?

Europe is tearing itself apart over the issue of race, nation and ethnicity. In this country past outbreaks of urban strife have failed to pin point an answer

4

to the question : who are the British? Ms Selvarajah is called a 'Paki'. A Sikh local government officer in Newcastle states that when he is asked where he is from, his listener does not want to hear 'Bradford' as the answer. A journalist in *The Guardian* recounts : 'A stall holder said to me "This is a good orange; you should know, where you come from." I said "What, east London?" (Phillips, 1992: 21). While our concept of British and British culture remains vague and undefined it is clear that the basic construction of Britishness excludes those who are not white.

We might consider the part played by ethnic monitoring in this debate. There is much argument about the value of collecting this data and whether it is collected period or whether any real steps to social reform are taken as a result of findings (Gordon, 1992). Here it is the categories offered for choice which are under scrutiny.

Consider the 1991 census. Respondents were asked to choose one of nine categories : White, Black Caribbean, Black African, Black other, Pakistani, Bangladeshi, Indian, Chinese, Other. These categories jumble together many different ideas about skin colour, about nationality, about ethnicity. How is a respondent meant to choose? The problems are illuminated by the following hypothetical example. Samina is a young woman born in Newcastle to parents who came to Tyneside in the early sixties from Pakistan. Considering that the question is asking about citizenship, Samina may choose 'Black other' reading this as Black British. The question may be asked as to why this is not specifically offered as a choice? Is this because the term 'Black British' seems to be a joining of two alien concepts? Samina may reject the term 'Black' as one which relates to an Afro-Caribbean experience because it draws attention by its polarising with white to the other polarisation of human and animal. In short it draws on the dehumanising experience of slavery and this was not the experience of Asian peoples. Thinking in this way leads Samina to where? Does she choose 'Pakistani' ? What does this category mean? Is it an expression of nationality in which case it does not fit Samina. Does it express cultural heritage or ethnicity as it is usually termed? What if Samina wears Western clothes, has English as her only language, has a British middle class lifestyle and does not consider herself to be a Muslim except in the nominal way that many British born white citizens would consider themselves to be Church of England? In what way is she 'Pakistani?' This leaves Samina with 'Other' as her only possible choice. Furthermore her choice of 'other' is not a fixed choice. The Runnymede Trust's research (Leech, 1989) reveals that in the United States, respondents commonly made new choices when subsequently asked the same question and offered the same list of categories. In Samina's case experiencing racism that limits her career choices or where she may live may cause her to reassess her identity. She may choose 'Black Other' as a personal affirmation of citizenship and an expression of political solidarity with others who have suffered white racism. She may choose 'Pakistani' on the grounds that in the eyes of the majority she will always be a foreigner.

Norman Tebbit talks about black people giving up and integrating into British society, well I did all that. I'm married to an English wife, I've accepted most of the values and yet I still get bricks thrown at me, I still get humiliated (BBC, 1991).

Black/immigrant/black

One route into the question of our nation's inability to absorb Black people as British lies perhaps in the arena of immigration controls and anti discrimination legislation.

While there has always been in and out migration in Britain it was during the period of the Second World War and just after, that immigration and race began to fuse together. From this time we see the confusion of the terms 'black' and 'immigrant'. This was already erroneous for some British cities had a long established black population. Liverpool is a prime example where the census of 1911 revealed 3,000 black citizens (Gifford, 1989: 28). Almost immediately the in-migration of black people became tied up in a game of numbers with debate as to how many constituted a problem, how many could be tolerated given the economic imperatives for more labour, how could people be excluded on the grounds of colour given the position of Britain as head of a Commonwealth both black and white. Hansard for 1958 captures the debate while *The Times* commenting on the 'race riots' (attacks by whites on blacks) reported the charges laid at the door of black people.

They are alleged to do no work and to collect a rich sum from the Assistance Board. They are said to find housing when white residents cannot. And they are charged with all kinds of misbehaviour, especially sexual (*The Times*, 3rd September, 1958 quoted in Solomos, 1989).

The first attempt to control immigration came in 1962 with the Commonwealth Immigrants Act's introduction of a system of work vouchers which intending immigrant workers had to obtain prior to entry. This act made no alteration to the position of dependents but fears that such changes would be made led to an increase in the number of women and children seeking entry prior to enactment. Such increases played into the hands of those who interpreted this as the shape of things to come.

The 1968 Commonwealth Immigrants Act is more note worthy for its process than its content. The Act was passed in parliament in three days to prevent African Asians exercising the right to enter: a right given as part of independence settlements. It introduced immigration control for Commonwealth citizens except for patrials (those with a parent or grandparent born in this country) and certain other groups and also put a limit on the number of work vouchers that might be issued.

The 1971 Immigration Act extended the deportation powers of the Home office already extended by the Immigration Appeals Act 1969. The 1971 Act is a major piece of immigration law: it repealed much of the 1962 and 1968 legislation by abolishing the system of work vouchers and thus effectively ending primary black immigration. From this time wives and dependents were to make up the major body of black immigrants. It should be noted that men who entered before enactment on January 1st 1973 were promised the automatic right to be joined by dependents. The 1988 Immigration Act revoked this right. The 1971 Act further revealed the racism underlying the law by giving white non-UK citizens more rights to enter and work in the UK than black UK citizens abroad who did not have a British parent or grandparent.

The final piece of legislation to date has been the British Nationality Act of 1981 which established three classes of citizenship and stated that citizenship could only be acquired by birth, descent or naturalisation. Eligibility for citizenship becomes largely confined to people born of British parents or parents who are settled here.

In 1991 the government has attempted to make legislation to reduce the number of refugees entering this country and it seems likely that this will emerge again as a political issue.

The shaping influence of the immigration legislation has been the view that only through strict control of black immigration can racial harmony be preserved. This is transparent in the famous speech of Margaret Thatcher in 1978.

... the British character has done so much for democracy, for law, and done so much throughout the world, that if there is any fear that it might be swamped, people are going to react and be rather hostile to those coming in. So if you want good race relations, you've got to allay people's fears on numbers (Thatcher, 1978).

Ruth Glass a decade earlier in her letter to *The Times* of August 5th 1967 laid bare the impact of such policies.

In the history of race relations in this country since the fifties, nothing has done more harm than the constantly reiterated demands to restrict entry of coloured immigrants - coupled, of course, with the exhortations to be fair to those who are already here. The demands have been accepted, not the exhortation. While coloured immigration has been restricted, race prejudice has grown. Indeed, it is such demands - never satisfied, following each restriction with a call for more - which have made colour prejudice respectable in Britain. "Stop coloured immigration". "Give these people their fares and send them home". "We don't want a half- caste Britain". A few years ago this was the language of political extremists at shabby street corners. Nowadays it is no longer surprising to hear it repeated almost word for word in statements issued from established quarters in Westminster (Glass, 1978).

Do these fears and demands simply create problems for the small number of new immigrants or does it undermine the position of all? Given the British confusion of black and immigrant and our unresolved concept of nation what can the impact of such words and such immigration acts be except to create division on a colour basis. For the black communities, the target of immigration controls, there is a growth in the climate of fear making even those settled legally afraid to claim benefits they are entitled or to complain about poor housing or low wages. For many in the white communities, black people can at best form only an underclass because They have come to take our jobs, our schools, our housing, welfare benefits built up on our contributions.

Such thinking leads inevitably to discrimination in service provision and delivery as well as violence arising from racial hatred which will be examined later in this chapter.

Since the mid sixties, Britain has chosen a particular policy response to the issue of discrimination. This was based on the view that eradication could be set in motion by legal sanctions and that the setting up of various welfare agencies would help immigrants adjust to 'British life'. Also dating from this time are the Section 11 posts set up under the Local Government Act 1966. These were available originally to certain local authorities and more lately to practically all, as a means of meeting the special needs of the black population. Since its inception there have been various criticisms of the use of section 11 ranging from the dead end career opportunities presented to black people by this mechanism to the 'gap filling' strategies of some local authorities faced by revenue cuts and redundancy of 'regular' staff.

In respect of legislation three successive acts have attempted to instigate social change.

The Race Relations Act of 1965 was limited in its scope - it made discrimination unlawful in places of public resort. It has been accused of ignoring the major areas of discrimination: what was important to quality of life was not being denied entry to a pub but being denied access to housing and to employment. While the shapers of the law had intended discrimination to be a criminal offence it was softened so that instead of being subject to police prosecution those who discriminated would be investigated by the newly constituted Race Relations Board which would attempt to gain compliance with the law.

The 1968 Race Relations Act came into being as a result of government research into the extent of discrimination. This emphasised that legislation must cover the most damaging areas of discrimination: housing, employment, insurance and credit facilities - that is cover the deficiencies of the 1965 Act. The Act also set up the Community Relations Commission intended to educate the country into harmonious relations.

The 1976 Act, the last and most far reaching, was heavily influenced by events in the United States and the recognition that discrimination existed not simply on a person to person basis but was entrenched in policy and practice. To this end the 1976 Act defined indirect discrimination that is practices which appeared to treat all the same but which militated against a particular group. The recently formed Race Relations Board and the Community Relations Commission were merged to make the Commission for Racial Equality. This was empowered to make formal investigations and issue non discrimination notices enforceable by court orders. In addition to alerting their local CRE those who felt they had been victims of discrimination were now able to take individual action through industrial tribunals.

The intention behind the merging of the RRB and the CRC was to give a more coherent approach to the law. Critics of the merger have stated that the result is confusion and a watering down of the punitive role. The trimming of budgets has left the CRE unable to investigate all but cases which it anticipates having the greatest public impact. Even where investigations are carried out, the example of Liverpool Housing Department found guilty of discrimination in 1984 and in 1989, suggests that the CRE's hope that investigation will be a spur to other local authorities to examine their policies and procedures (CRE, 1989) is a triumph of hope over experience.

Why then has the regulatory mechanism had such poor impact? Each of the Acts can be criticised for weak penalties and the failure to make discrimination into a criminal act: it remains a tort (that is a civil wrong). The tenor of all three acts has been to create a climate in which discrimination would be inhibited by a growing awareness of wrong doing and the human right to equality rather than to uncover and punish discrimination.

Is this enough? The CRE in their second review of the Race Relations Act 1976 reveal a deep sense of frustration with the scope of the legislation and their own powers to act.

While there is no evidence that the racial discrimination covered by the Race Relations Act 1976 which the Commission tackles through its law enforcement powers is increasing, it is not decreasing at all fast enough. By contrast, there is this upsurge in criminal racial harassment and violence, which is beyond the Commission's powers to deal with directly. What is the difference? Does it lie in the vigour of the law enforcement or in the situation of the offenders? Is racial discrimination practised by those with economic power in society, and racial harassment and violence practised by those without it? Those with economic power would obviously feel more secure than those without it and have no need to find scapegoats for their own situation.

In the case of racial discrimination, those in positions of power and authority... are in a position to adopt, implement and monitor the kind of comprehensive equal opportunity policies that would put an end to discrimination and enable all our citizens to realise their full potential and make their full contribution to society regardless of their ethnic origins. That racial discrimination still exists at substantial levels indicates that far too few have done so (CRE, 1991: 16-17).

Legal change may not necessarily create social change. Lustgarten and Edwards (1992) argue that the law is weakened because of the British adherence to individualism. In the USA if an employer is found to have discriminated against a black person the same employer is liable to pay compensation to all those persons in that class: a substantial financial penalty. In the UK the employer pays the individual who brought the action and with compensation levels set low 'by making discrimination cheap [English law] virtually ensures the ineffectiveness of the rights approach' (Lustgarten and Edwards, 1992: 274). Similarly those employers found guilty of refusing a black person a job or promotion are not then set targets for the employment and promotion of black people. This highlights also the difference between the British emphasis on positive action and the American reliance on positive discrimination in the form of quotas based on labour market percentages.

9

It might also be argued that for the most part the issue of inequality lies beyond the scope of legal change, while direct discrimination may be a matter for law, the deeper structural issues leading to racial disadvantage are areas not for legal change but for political and administrative change.

The role of local government

To consider administrative change is to examine the part played by local government. Why local government has taken on this role can be interpreted in a number of ways. It could be action in the face of central government apathy and the poor legal framework. For those urban areas which suffered unrest in the 1980s, positive measures could be seen as a self defence mechanism. The motivation might be political in that local politicians need to improve their power base. The measures taken can also be interpreted as responses to section 71 of the 1976 Race Relations Act which lays an injunction on local authorities that:

> Without prejudice to their obligations to comply with any other provision of this Act, it shall be the duty of every local authority to make appropriate arrangements with a view to securing their functions are carried out with regard to the need: (a) to eliminate unlawful racial discrimination; and (b) to promote equality of opportunity, and good relations, between persons of different racial groups.

Local authorities have responded in a variety of ways:

• in Education, the development of new teaching materials, the development of new perspectives and expectations among teachers.

• in Housing, the introduction of anti-harassment clauses in tenancy agreements, the monitoring of housing procedures.

• in Social Services, the tackling of best practice issues in the adoption and fostering of black children, the recognition of the different needs of black elderly people.

• in Environmental Health / Public Protection the setting up of panels and discussion groups to create understanding between restaurant owners and officers.

• in Planning the recognition of the need to plan for different cultural needs and the targeting of grants at black businesses.

In all sectors of local government there have been employment initiatives. These range from the liberal targeted training schemes such as Positive Action Training in Housing (PATH) to the more radical stance which sees the traditional reliance on certain qualification and levels of experience as excluding black people who may have followed other career paths.

Some of these initiatives attracted vehement media attention particularly in the field of anti racist education. Robin Richardson of Brent commenting on these views remarks that:

There was the assertion of white cultural hegemony (what *The Daily Telegraph* called "the British educational ethos") against the Labour politicians of Brent, whose menace was deemed to lie not only or even primarily in the fact that they were Labour but in the fact that they were to a large extent black. It is essential to note this respect that the *Evening Standard* felt quite tolerant towards Labour politicians in Ealing, Camden and Islington since these were, it said, white and middle-class. White people are merely "loony left": black people, however, it was subliminally implied in the *Express*, *Mail* and *Telegraph*, are "evil". This was traditional white racist demonology. What was relatively new, in the press reporting about the DPRE [Development Programme for Racial Equality], was the identification of black people with Stalinist tyrannies in Eastern Europe. It was a potent way not only of emphasising their "devilry" but also of suggesting their treacherous unreliability as citizens, and of giving voice to the suspicion that they were not really British (Richardson, 1991).

Vitriolic publicity combining with revenue cutbacks has resulted in equal opportunities work sinking to a lower profile. For those committed to a multi-racial Britain with equality as a foundation stone there seems a bleak future. The present government is wedded to an enterprise culture which holds up for praise the Mr Patel who makes his million and suggests that the Mr Patel who complains of being blocked by racism is a victim of his own idleness. Further legislation seems unlikely and attempts in 1986 to introduce a Racial Harassment Bill which would define harassment as an offence and provide penalties for perpetrators was defeated.

Racial harassment

Type	Frequency			
	Almost Daily	Monthly	Several times pa	Never
Walking past graffiti	14%	15%	28%	42%
Personal abuse	12%	14%	31%	43%
Attacks on property	5%	8%	31%	55%
Threatening behaviour	5%	10%	16%	69%
Bodily harm	2%	1%	7%	89%

(Source: Newcastle MBC, 1990)

Racial harassment is a grim reminder for all black citizens irrespective of class that they are not welcome.

Location and concentration seem to play no part. Racial harassment is as common an occurrence for black citizens in Newcastle as it is for those in Newham (CRE, 1987).

No doubt there are many other cities which could produce worse figures but Newcastle has a very small black population (4%) and is famed for friendliness or so the popular image proclaims.

It is sobering to consider that Liverpool arouses the same warm feelings:

... I have found the city to be uniquely generous, uniquely hospitable, uniquely tolerant. Because of its history... there has been an appreciation on the part of Liverpool people of what it is to be in a minority, and often therefore people will reach out to provide a helping hand (David Alton in Gifford et al, 1989: 81).

This needs to be set against the Liverpool 8 Inquiry's Declaration of Principles:

After nine days of hearing evidence, holding private meetings and visiting centres of activity, the Inquiry team feels compelled to express its shock at the prevalence in Liverpool of racial attitudes, racial abuse and racial violence directed against black citizens of the city.

Time and again the Inquiry has been informed that black adults, black youth and even black children have to face open expressions of racism (Gifford, 1989: 22).

The truth is as Salman Rushdie wrote ten years ago that 'very few white people, except those active in fighting racism, are willing to believe the descriptions of contemporary reality offered by blacks' (Rushdie, 1982).

Conclusion

Britain appears to be in an impasse. That racism is alive and well and kicking is obvious yet we seem not to know how to tackle it or is it that we have ceased to care? Central government continues to ignore the race question while local authorities coping with cuts in capital and revenue are hampered from building on the initiatives of earlier years. Yet there is still money and new mechanisms for improving the quality of life for black citizens. New initiatives such as City Challenge seem to be based on an acknowledgement that trickle down effects have not occurred and that what is needed is partnership with communities as well as the business world. The challenge for local authorities remains that with such evidence of deprivation in the black communities there needs to be a concerted gearing of funding to these communities. The problem remains that with so little money to spend, there is more awareness of who benefits. This no doubt leads to anxiety about a white backlash but to act in this fear is to collude with those who deny black people citizenship.

Local government can only play a small part in affirming black citizenship by targeted spending and practices free of discrimination. There is a role for every agency, every business and for central government if we are to see equality across the board and now. Anything less is tokenism.

References

British Broadcasting Corporation, (1991), "Who's Batting for Britain".

Commission for Racial Equality (1987), *Living In Terror*, CRE, London.

Commission for Racial Equality (1989), "Liverpool Guilty of Race Bias", Press Release, 25th May.

Commission for Racial Equality (1991), *Second Review of the Race Relations Act 1976*, CRE, London.

Gifford, Lord and Brown, W. and Bundey, R. (1989), *Loosen the Shackles*, Keria Press, London.

Glass, Ruth (1967), Letter, *The Times*, 5th August.

Gordon, P. (1992), "The Racialization of Statistics" in Skellington R. with Morris P., *Race in Britain Today*, Sage, London.

Inside Housing (1992), 29th May.

Leech, K. (1989), *A Question in Dispute: the Debate about an "ethnic" question in the Census*, Runnymede Trust, London.

Lustgarten, L. and Edwards, J. (1992), "Racial inequality and the limits of law" in Braham, P. and Rattansi, A. and Skellington, R. (eds) *Racism and Anti racism: Inequalities, Opportunities and Policies*, Sage, London.

Newcastle MBC (1990), Minority Ethnic Communities Survey 1990, Racial Equality Sub-Committee, 21st November.

Newcastle University (1992), Newcastle's West End. Monitoring the City Challenge Initiative: A Base Line report, Newcastle University, Newcastle.

Philips, M. (1992), "Surely you can't be the barrister?", *The Guardian*, 1st July.

Ratcliffe, P. (1992), "Renewal, regeneration and `race': Issues in urban policy", *New Community*, 18 (3) April: 387-400.

Richardson, R. (1991), "Brent - Development Programme for Racial equality" in Race Equality and Training into the 1990s, Proceedings of Mosaic Conference, BBC Education, London.

Rutherford School (1992), Verbal Presentation to Newcastle City Challenge West End Partnership Meeting, 18th June.

Selvarajah, S. (1992), *The Guardian*, 8th April: 11.

Solomos, J. (1989), *Race and Racism in Contemporary Britain*, Macmillan, London.

Thatcher, M, (1978), Granada Television, 30th January.

Chapter 2

Gender and sexuality

Sexism

Sexism affects all women in all aspects of their lives because it prescribes the roles and behaviour that are deemed to be acceptable (Dutta and Taylor, 1989).

The mystery of the invisible woman

Woman's invisibility arises from a number of quarters: language, lack of data, lack of power and concepts of 'femininity' which say that women ought to be passive, docile and dependent. The same view sees a woman's natural place as being in the home (that is out of public life) where she has a specific set of tasks which are thought to be universal because they are based on biological differences (Dutta and Taylor, 1989).

One of the most insidious attacks is from language. Over the past few years a number of expressions have become politically incorrect: the use of the word 'chairman' which assumes that the post holder should be a man or 'madam chairman' suggesting that a woman will operate in an amateurish fashion. There are many everyday examples: it is more common for women to have 'Ms' offered as a title parallelling them with men whose title does not reveal their marital status. The new man may be rebelling against ingrained sexism but has there really been an attitude change? Women may no longer hear dehumanising and insulting expressions such as 'bird', 'chick', 'bit of skirt', 'tart', used to their face but does this mean they are on the way out? Perhaps there is progress but consider the still widespread use of 'man' as a so called generic term. Research has shown that the word 'man' is generally understood to be gender specific; in other words the word conjures up a man not humanity. The pronoun 'he' operates in the same way, being used to convey humankind but setting in the mind a male figure.

Sexist language is any item of language which through its structure or use, constitutes a male as norm view of society by trivialising, insulting or rendering women invisible (Robertson and Mills, undated).

The male as norm view is further supported by lack of data about women. Research often fails to pick up on the gender element suggesting that the experience of women is the same as that of men. These issues will be further explored in the policy chapters which follow. The imperative is for research which brings to light the impact of policy and practices upon women. The following suggestions are taken from a European Foundation report on women and they put forward an agenda for research:

• To what extent does each research area carry out analysis on how women are represented in its areas of concern, for example, the gender composition of safety committees, the male and female composition of shift workers or homeless youth.
• To what extent does the analysis of the provision of services (for example, public services) within each area take into account the gender profile of users and the specific needs of women as users.
• Does the research address the possible legal and institutional forms of discrimination based on gender affecting its area (for example within social security systems).
• Has the analysis explored the barriers (for example social attitudes or the availability of child care facilities) which might affect female participation or the lack of participation in specific activities).
• Has the question of positive discrimination (for example, with regard to training in new technologies, career development, participation) in favour of women been considered?
• What kind of future trends are emerging (for example, on the labour market or within polarising urban areas) and are these being analysed on a male / female basis (Barry and Kelleher, 1991).

It remains true that where research has identified the particular problems of women there is not a guaranteed response to the issue. An outstanding example is the growth of poverty among women. Two decades ago the poorest people were the elderly, the majority of which are women, while now the poorest are single mothers and their children. In this country there are more than one million single mothers making up one seventh of all households: over two thirds of these are in the poverty trap. This situation has been exacerbated by the action and inaction of government. Many of the benefits which these women rely on such as child benefit have come under attack with a refusal to link child benefits to either inflation or wage increases. Emerging arguments about the 'underclass' often blame single mothers for undermining society, a crime which can be punished by benefits cuts (Redding, 1990).

A case taken to the European Court of Justice in 1992 is an interesting exploration of how changes to social security may militate against women.

Nine judges in Luxembourg rejected claims by Patricia Cresswell and Sonia Jackson that the Government's refusal to allow child care expenses to be deducted in calculating their benefit breached EC directives on social security and equal access to work, and directly discriminated against women. Ms Cresswell brought her case after discovering she was £10 per week poorer working part-time than relying solely on state benefits. Until April 1988, low earners could claim supplementary benefit as an income top-up, and child care costs could be deducted in calculating benefit, child-minding ceased to be deductible. The judges ruled yesterday that the directives did not apply to supplementary benefit or income support. To fall within the 1979 directive on equal treatment of men and women in social security matters, judges said, the scheme would have to protect against one of five risks: sickness, invalidity, old age, accidents at work and occupational diseases, or unemployment. The directive did not cover a statutory scheme designed to top up an income below the individual's needs. Nor did the scheme fall within the 1976 directive on equal access to employment, promotion, and training. It was intended to provide support for people with insufficient means, and was not concerned with access to employment or working conditions (Dyer, 1992).

New policies such as Community Care push an increasing burden upon families, which usually means women, to care for elderly relatives. The same women who may be looking after children and / or going out to work. The misconceptions about elderly Asian people and their families 'natural desire to care for them at home' as well as lack of sensitivity to cultural differences where provision is made may create greater burdens for black women and their families.

Women's schooling (EOC, 1991) and domestic circumstances leave them with lower earning power than men and more limited job opportunities (Holdsworth, 1988).

The exclusion of women will be explored throughout the book examining how male planners plan for male use though the end consumer may be female, and how a male dominated view of work and workers may serve to keep women out or out of the top jobs.

Violence against women

As with the operation of all discriminations, sexism also seeks to oppress not only through stereotyping and exclusion but also through violence which takes many forms. The obvious example is the woman who suffers at the hands of a violent partner. Domestic violence is a major cause of women's homelessness and yet the spread of refuges (about 200 across the country with ten or so for black women and few giving access to disabled women) remains inadequate and the funding of these hostels and their workers is unstable. Pat Niner's work on homeless practice demonstrated that while women with children fleeing violence were seen by local authorities as an automatic priority for rehousing under homeless legislation, those without children were not (Niner, 1989). In short women are often only valued when they are mothers. It remains true that women without financial resources of their own and without friends or family to take them in are frequently unable to separate from their partner.

Women who have come to this country to marry a British national find themselves ground between two stones if their partner is violent. The Home Office threatens to deport such women if they have entered the country within the last twelve months. The effect is to place pressure upon women to stay in violent households at the risk of injury or death and effectively encourages the men to be as violent as they like (Everywoman, 1992:5).

Another route is to secure the assistance of the police but they are reluctant to involve themselves.

As long as terms such as "it's only a domestic" are allowed to prevail the task of improving the lot of battered women will be greater (Nottinghamshire County Council, 1988).

Domestic violence has been highlighted in the press through the campaigning for Sara Thornton and the re-opening of the Kiranjit Ahluwalia case. Ms Ahluwalia was sentenced to life imprisonment after she murdered her violent husband who had systematically abused her for ten years. The fact that she was an abused wife was not allowed to be sufficient provocation given that her 'retaliation' was not immediate. These instances can be compared with the case of Joseph McGrail who beat and kicked his drunken wife to death yet walked free with a suspended sentence after the judge commented that the dead wife 'would have tried the patience of a saint'. Douglas Coles killed his wife because 'she was neurotic and nagged and he snapped'. He was sentenced to two years probation (Phillips, 1991).

The issue of criminal justice is interesting for the majority of crime is committed by men (eighty three per cent in fact) and more than half of these by boys aged between 14 and 18. There are thirty six times more men than women serving sentences for violent or sexual crimes yet women, who rarely commit this type of offence, are more likely to be sent to prison than a man. It also is true that black men are more likely to be sent to prison than white and that the greatest risk of imprisonment is faced by black women who make up only two per cent of the country's population but twenty four per cent of the female prison population. Thirty per cent of adult women in prison are there on a first conviction compared to only nine per cent of the male prison population. Women are also diagnosed as psychiatric cases and sent to maximum security hospitals at seven times the rate of men. Dr Gillian Mezey quoted in Angela Phillips' article feels that this is because when a woman has committed a crime which is regarded as incompatible with her female status, she has not only transgressed against the criminal law

... she has transgressed against the code of what it is to be female - docile, passive and gentle. She may be regarded as doubly bad and put in prison for a long time or, if she is not bad, she must be very, very mad and in need of psychiatric treatment.

It remains true that the legal process is in the hands of men and that change is only likely to happen if and when women are seen more frequently in the court room as barristers and more importantly as judges.

On the issue of rape while there are signs that the police are taking a more sensitive approach through the introduction of specially trained women officers and counselling rooms with soft furnishing, the legal process may cause her suffering and humiliation (the giving of evidence in open court). Frequently the sentences given to rapists and those guilty of sexual assault are derisory

The case of Sir Harold Cassel who put a man on probation for sexually molesting his twelve year old step-daughter. He felt that attack was at least partly justified because the child's mother was pregnant and this precipitated "a lack of sexual appetite in the lady and considerable problems for a healthy young husband" (Phillips, 1991: 27).

The spread of Rape Crisis centres, like women's refuges, remains poor.

... there is currently funding for only two full time workers at the Rape Crisis Centre, to cover the whole of the West Midlands. Last year 500 attacks on women were reported to the Centre. There were no doubt many more. In addition, hundreds of women are still quietly suffering the after-effects of past rapes and assaults (Birmingham City Council, 1990).

Violence takes many forms including sexual harassment which is now coming to light as an issue for action by trade unions and employers alike. Sexual harassment in the form of dirty jokes, personal remarks, pornographic pictures and groping is used by men of power to threaten, humiliate and patronise women causing loss of mental and physical well being.

Two steps forward - one step back?

Thanks to the Women's Movement, attitudes are different: the language is less patronising; women are tolerated - if not welcomed - in places previously forbidden to them. Political parties, banks, industry now take women more seriously and so do women themselves. They have become more assertive and confident. Yet it is still true that rich men have the best of all worlds and poor women the worst. There are few women at the top in industry or any of the professions and remarkably few in Parliament. Despite the example of a woman prime minister and the best endeavours of the 300 Group to fill half the House of Commons with women, only six per cent of MPs are women (Holdsworth, 1988).

Much has been achieved in the field of women's struggle for equality:

• discriminatory procedures have been rooted out in recruitment, selection and promotion.

- there have been improvements in the provision of work place nurseries though these are initiatives taken by employers since government refuses to take responsibility.

- there has been a growth of women only transport projects.

- targeted education and leisure initiatives.

- shoppers creches are more common though far from universal.

- there has been increased support for women's organisations and the establishment of women's units within local authorities.

Yet as the quotation reminds us the visibility of women has not increased greatly and decision makers with power over men and women are likely to be men.

Given that the credit for much of the progress can be claimed by local authorities it is worrying that in the endless round of cuts it is initiatives for women which may suffer. Haringey LBC which is one of the most advanced local authorities in equal opportunities work was operating for a period in 1991 under a Section 114 order which prohibits spending not considered essential by the District Auditor. Women's equality initiatives were practically halted as a result (Cooper, 1991). In other local authorities the prospects of further work is probably dominated by cuts in budgets creating marginalisation and reduction in scope of activity and this at a time when Compulsory Competitive Tendering may lead to exploitation of women manual workers; cuts in services hit the poorest in our communities often elderly women and single mothers; the financial starving of voluntary organisations leads to loss of services and many women's jobs. As Angela Holdsworth comments,' the battle is far from over'.

Heterosexism

Homosexual: pansy, fairy, queer, pervert, lesbian, dyke (Roget's Thesaurus).

Heterosexism is a system of ideas and practices based on a set of beliefs about heterosexuality being the normal and natural sexuality for both women and men, and all other sexual practices, in particular homosexuality, being deviant. Heterosexism lays down the rules and conditions under which all sexualities are valued or devalued in our society, and penalties / benefits accordingly awarded. Under heterosexism, lesbians and gay men are particularly penalised (Egerton et al, undated).

While there has never been a time in British society when homosexuality was totally accepted it was only in the last hundred years that the law has taken any great interest in same sex relations between men. Prior to Labouchere's amendment to the 1885 Criminal Justice Act which made unlawful 'indecent acts' between men there were only ancient penalties for the 'abominable crime of buggery' which had been used to curb the activities of less discreet male prostitutes and what would be termed public indecency.

The Labouchere amendment opened the doors to the prosecution of any homosexual man no matter how discreet his lifestyle and of course to the blackmailing of rich men with public positions to protect. The most famous example is Oscar Wilde, sent to prison for two years with hard labour (Fido, 1973).

Between the 1890s with the furore caused by the Wilde trial and the late 1950s, to be a gay man was to wear a public face of heterosexuality while often pursuing a furtive sex life. The deep public distaste of same sex relationships caused men to resort to cottaging that is the picking up of casual sexual partners in public lavatories. Then as now this was a practice fraught with danger since the practice remains unlawful and the police in certain forces are known to act as *agent provocateurs* (Humphries, 1988).

The prosecution of gay men has seen peaks and troughs: with the fifties and the Guy Burgess spy scandal and its associations with homosexuality triggering a zealous campaign by the police. Gay men were one of the groups persecuted by the Third Reich though their suffering is much less well documented than that of the Jewish people.

There have never been laws against same sex relations between women possibly because of ancient thoughts about the sin of 'spilling seed' and the idea that women's sexuality was a matter of passivity and little if any pleasure. Stigmatization of lesbians became more apparent in the twenties with the publication of Radclyffe Hall's book 'The Well of Loneliness' which introduced the word 'lesbian' into common parlance.

The moves to destigmatise same sex orientation began with the change to the law in 1967 (Sexual Offences Act) which sanctioned sexual relations between consenting adult (21 years old) men in private. While other countries in Europe have introduced the same age of consent for opposite and same sex relationships, Britain has yet to re-examine the issue. More powerful shock waves were caused by the American movement to establish group identity and a positive image through the word 'gay' and phrases such as 'glad to be gay' parallelling 'black is beautiful'. The growing assertiveness of gay people and, in particular, the coming out of Peter Tatchell, a Labour parliamentary candidate for Bermondsey in the by election of 1982, resulted in the Labour party taking up the inequalities suffered by gay men and lesbians though these initiatives were much later than their adherence to equal opportunities for black people and for women. While the Labour party officially backed anti discrimination work and positive action, few local authorities made any undertaking to this group perhaps fearing the reaction of the press which was quick to label as 'Loony Left' those who espoused this cause. The Local Government Act 1988 with its famous clause 28 making unlawful acts of local authorities to 'promote homosexuality' provoked the last large scale demonstration in support of gay and lesbian rights.

Whether there has been a national change of heart on same sex relationships is difficult to assert. It remains true that 'coming out' is more acceptable for actors, musicians and those in the theatrical world than in many other walks of life. Is this really a great advance since the theatrical and artistic community has always been the one which absorbed many whose dress and behaviour may have been judged as 'effeminate' or 'mannish' by usual standards? It remains true that 'coming out' for many gay men and lesbians results in pressure to leave a job (in the armed forces homosexuality is illegal and results in dismissal) and the risk of harassment by others who see their relationships and preferences as an aberration.

Public attitudes about homosexuality have moved through the spectrum of being first a moral problem, then a legal one, finally a medical problem and then simply a biological phenomenon (Oliver 1990). Recent American research has now indicated that certain nerve clusters in the brain are larger in homosexual men than in heterosexual though results are less conclusive in the case of lesbians and heterosexual women. While this backs up the idea that sexual orientation is born not made, which has been continually asserted by gays and lesbians, it may also suggest that since a cause has been found there may be a cure (Reed, 1992).

While many gay men and lesbians are now more open about their sexuality and life style, homosexuality remains secret and shrouded in ignorance. There is no doubt that in matters of sexuality there should be respect for all who do not harm or exploit others, but legislation, housing policies, policy and practice in respect of adoption and fostering, continue to ignore or militate against those whose sexual preference is for their own sex.

References

Barry, U. and Kelleher, P. (1991), *Review of the Foundation's work 1985-1992 and it's Implications for Women*, European Foundation for the Improvement of Living and Working Conditions, Dublin.

Birmingham City Council (1990), Women in the Centre: Women, Planning and Birmingham City Centre, Birmingham.

Cooper, D. (1991), Equal Opportunities Work: After the boom, the doom and gloom, *Everywoman*, April: 16-17.

Dutta, R. and Taylor, G. (1989), *Housing Equality*, CHAR, London.

Dyer, C. (1992), "Single mothers lose child care claim", *The Guardian*, 17th July: 4.

Egerton, J.; Hemmings, S.; Henry, S.; Lewis, A.; Oram, G.; Parmar, P and Robertson, H. (undated), "Danger! Heterosexism at Work", Industry and Employment Branch of the Greater London Council, London.

Equal Opportunities Commission (1991), *Equal Opportunities in Schools: A Guide for School Governors*, Equal Opportunities Commission.

Everywoman (1992), July / August: 5.

Fido, M. (1973), *Oscar Wilde*, Cardinal, Sphere Books, London.

Holdsworth, A. (1989), *Out of the Doll's House*, BBC Books, London

Humphries, S. (1988), *The Secret World of Sex*, Sidgwick and Jackson, London.

Niner, P. (1989), *Homelessness in Nine Local Authorities*, HMSO, London.

Nottinghamshire County Council (1988), Report of the Domestic Violence Panel.

Oliver, M. (1990), *The Politics of Disablement*, Macmillan, London.

Phillips, A. (1991), "Rough Justice", *Elle*, December: 27-29.

Redding, D. (1990), "Blaming it on the mothers", *Community Care*, 23rd August.

Reed, C. (1992), "Homosexuals are born not made", *The Guardian*, 3rd August.

Robertson, S. and Mills, S. (undated) "Gender-free language: Guide-lines for the use of staff and students", University of Strathclyde.

Chapter 3

Discrimination against the disabled

You've got this woman in a wheelchair trying to get into a building, but there's a flight of steps. A woman comes past, takes a look at her and says "Oh dear, she's ill. What a shame, she can't get into the building". Well I've seen medical conditions that cause you to have rashes, I've come across medical conditions that give you headaches, I've come across medical conditions that give you spots before the eyes, but I've never before seen a medical condition that builds flights of stairs (Sutherland, 1990).

Definitions and models

Every discussion of disability begins with the same question: who are the disabled? In discussing gender, the world is split simply into male and female. Below this simplicity many men and women might find themselves at variance with prevalent concepts of 'masculinity' and 'femininity'. Other men and women whose behaviour, dress and relationships don't conform to heterosexual models may find themselves the target of discrimination in all its forms. How men and women are gendered is a matter for debate and research; sex, however, is almost always a matter of biological fact, not one of conjecture.

In discussing race, societies can be pictured as made up of myriad ethnic groups, the members of which share a common cultural heritage. Some of these ethnic groups will be viewed as minorities which of course has nothing to do with numbers and everything to do with power. The minority groups are not people 'like us' and though they display a wide variety of physical appearance, of language, of religious beliefs they share a common experience of discrimination. In this respect the world divides into those ethnic groups who suffer discrimination and those who are in power. Events in central Europe and the Middle East demonstrate that in some parts of the world ethnicity is the determining factor while, in this country, colour and the ghosts of old colonialism are dominant.

How does disability fit into this picture? Is it that disability like sex is a biological fact or is it that, like ethnicity we all have some impairment but only some groups suffer discrimination? The question may be asked - why do we need a definition at all?

- In a perfect world there would be good access in its myriad forms for all

- adaptable housing

- user friendly and affordable transport

- a built environment which caters for all

- an integrated education system helping children and adults of all abilities

- the eradication of supply side and demand side difficulties leading to a level playing field of competition in the job market

- a community care service which was moulded round citizen needs

- participation in decision making for all.

Yes, it's a long shopping list but most people in Britain take these rights for granted.

Our far from perfect world distributes welfare benefits according to degree of disability, segregates disabled children into special schools and often discriminates against those job applicants who declare they are 'registered disabled'. Where the line is drawn between 'normality' and 'disability' and who draws the line are matters of vital importance.

How can a line be drawn? Look at yourself and the people around you. Some of us are born with severe impairment such as no arms or legs. Some are left handed and spend their lives frustrated by scissors, tin openers - the right but wrong handedness of the world. Others may suffer a sudden change brought about by a road or sporting accident or a stroke which brings paralysis or loss of speech, while others may contract a progressive disease such as MS and find themselves coping with mobility or sensory impairment. Many have none of this to contend with but may still find it more difficult to climb the stairs as they grow older, hold the paper further away to read as sight alters and complain that everyone mumbles as hearing changes. A life event for many women is pregnancy and during the later months will curse turnstiles, pause for breath on steep streets and search in growing discomfort for a public toilet. How many of these people are disabled? Selwyn Goldsmith, in his influential 'Designing for the Disabled' says that the disabled are only turned into the handicapped by their environment. On this definition all these people are handicapped. Are they also disabled? No one will label a pregnant woman disabled and most of the common infirmities of getting older are not classified as disabilities.

This quick tour of the population illustrates that most people are impaired or will be because the essence of human life is change. Given our changing condition where is the line to be drawn between the disabled and others? Various bodies have presented definitions of disability, this is the widely accepted one offered by the World Health Organisation.

Impairment: Any loss or abnormality of psychological, physiological or anatomical structure or function.

Disability: Any restriction or lack (resulting from an impairment) of ability to perform an activity in the manner or within the range considered normal for a human being.

Handicap: A disadvantage for a given individual resulting from an impairment or disability that limits the fulfilment of a role for that individual. The role will depend on age, sex, social and cultural factors.

The first definition talks about the parts of the body or the systems which don't work at all or as they should. This concept of impairment covers a wide range. Many people have impaired sight but there is a great difference between those who are blind and those for whom the wearing of spectacles and contact lenses has eradicated any restriction. Impairment does not automatically lead to disability which describes activities and functions that cannot be done because of impairment. If the first two are not automatically linked what of the second two? Consider a person whose impairment is that they have no legs. This person is disabled according to the WHO definition because they cannot move about in the normal manner; are they then handicapped by which the WHO means that they will have problems in relationships and with the environment. The answer is that they will but consider how the handicap arises. The WHO definition, while recognising that disability has social dimensions sees the handicap as arising from the individual and his / her condition (Oliver, 1990; Lonsdale, 1990). Consider the following extract from Oliver Sachs perceptive exploration of deafness 'Seeing Voices':

Through a mutation, a recessive gene brought out by inbreeding, a form of hereditary deafness existed for 250 years on Martha's Vineyard, Massachusetts, following the arrival of the first settlers in the 1690s. By the mid-nineteenth century, scarcely an up-island family was unaffected, and in some villages (Chilmark, West Tisbury), the incidence of deafness had risen to one in four. In response to this, the entire community learned Sign, and there was free and complete intercourse between the hearing and the deaf. Indeed the deaf were scarcely seen as "deaf" and certainly not seen as being at all "handicapped".

In the astonishing interviews recorded by Groce, the island's older residents would talk at length, vividly and affectionately about their former relatives, neighbors, and friends, usually without even mentioning that they were deaf. And it would only be if this question was specifically asked that there would be a pause and then, "Now you come to mention it, yes, Ebenezer **was** deaf and dumb". But Ebenezer's deaf and dumbness had never set him apart, had scarcely even been noticed as such: he had been seen, he was remembered, simply as "Ebenezer" - friend, neighbor, dory fisherman - not as some special, handicapped, set apart deaf mute (Sachs, 1991: 32-33).

From this a new perspective emerges on disability which is clarified by the definition put forward by UPIAS (Union of Physically Impaired Against Segregation).

Impairment: lacking part or all of a limb, or having a defective limb, organism or mechanism of the body.

Disability: the disadvantage or restriction of activity caused by a contemporary social organisation which takes no or little account of people who have physical impairments and thus excludes them from the mainstream of social activities.

Two important differences emerge between this and the WHO definition. Firstly the term 'handicap' has been dropped; a term which Colin Barnes (1991:2) dismisses as having associations with 'cap in hand' and begging. This is an image which will be explored later. The second difference is in emphasis. The Who definition focuses on what is wrong with the individual and suggests that disadvantage arises naturally from the condition of being not like 'us'. The UPIAS view is that to have a physical disability is to be in a minority group in society whose needs are ignored and whose physical appearance may lead to being treated as less equal.

These differences can be seen as springing from two models of thinking about disability: the medical and the social. The medical model focuses on a person's medical condition or impairment defining them as 'ill' and therefore unable to participate in the full range of human activities. It fails to take a holistic view: it sees not the person but a pair of defective eyes or as a leg that will not bend. The social model sees the problem lying not with the disabled person but with the able bodied in society who have discriminated against disabled people in the field of employment, of education, and in the built environment. These primary handicaps frequently lead to the secondary handicap of poverty (Lonsdale, 1991; Barnes, 1991). The social model states that if discriminatory practice was recognised for what it was and eradicated then, disabled people could be valuable members of society with much to contribute.

The second section examines what it is like to be disabled: in what ways are people socialised into the role of a disabled person, what images are associated with disability, what language is used to dismiss or empower?

Language and images

Just as definition is a problem so is language. Consider the terms used to classify disabled people. Frequently they are divided into categories which denote their particular impairment: the blind, the deaf, the non ambulant. Such labels convey the idea of different impairments which may have different impacts on individuals and may call forth very different responses from the able bodied. The blind always summon up pity while deaf people are frequently dismissed as stupid. This kind of labelling is impersonal but also denies what Susan Lonsdale (1990: 34) calls the 'ubiquity of disability', the stigma, exclusion, discrimination and dependency and is therefore part of the medical model.

There are other terms. Remember the childhood insult 'Spacka' deriving from spastic and being used to mean stupid. The American 'dumb' is in the same mode. 'Cripple' is insulting though it is worth considering this provocative piece by Robert Ilson (1992: 19):

[Cripple] is easy to criticise because it can be, and has been, used as an insult. Its defence is the courage required to use it of oneself, acknowledging the anguish as the first step to transcending it. That is the courage of the sort that members of the religious Society of Friends required in order to accept the name "Quakers"; that strong women required in order to take pride in being "viragos"; that blacks required in order to reclaim their colour as their name. "Crip", an intimately familiar shortening of "cripple", goes further still in displaying a cocky readiness to stand up to whatever circumstances or ignorance can dish out.

For many commentators there is the debate as to whether the correct term is 'disabled people' or 'people with disabilities'. What do we make of the American 'physically challenged' or 'differently abled'? Susan Lonsdale (1990) prefers 'people with disabilities' because it retains the concept of disability without suggesting that a person's disability encompasses all there is to know about that individual. The alternative view is this:

It is sometimes argued, often by able-bodied professionals and some disabled people, that "people with disabilities" is the preferred term, for it asserts the value of the person first and the disability then becomes merely an appendage. This liberal and humanist view flies in the face of reality as it is experienced by disabled people themselves who argue that far from being an appendage, disability is an essential part of the self. in this view it is nonsensical to talk about the person and the disability separately and consequently disabled people are demanding acceptance as they are, as disabled people (Oliver, 1990: xiii).

Micheline Mason, a disability equality trainer, rejects the so called 'politically correct' terms saying:

My disability is a fundamental factor in the being that is "me". I do not want to deny this by calling myself a "person with special needs" or any other euphemism, nor do I want to deny the collective identity we have achieved for ourselves. therefore I am a disabled person, and proud of it (Mason, 1992: 20).

The two points to be made about language is firstly that it is important for disabled people that they can take control of their own lives which includes having the right to name yourself. The second point is that by opening up the debate on language, society may begin to explore the attitudes which are given voice by certain words and phrases and from this clearer perception may come action.

Language and images are linked. The word 'handicapped' is derived from 'cap in hand' and suggests the beggar, the object of charity.

I really like those collecting boxes that stand in shop doors, the kind with models of disabled people with holes in their head. I've always thought, when I was little I used to think that's how you could tell a disabled person, they've got a big slot in their head for putting money into (Sutherland, 1990).

A friend of mine, she was once shopping in Leeds with an able-bodied, non-disabled person. She uses an electric wheelchair, she has no arms or legs, operates the wheelchair with her shoulder. She was stopped at a corner with a friend, drinking a can of coke and a woman walked up to her, spoke a few words and dropped some money into her can of coke and walked away (Chapman quoted in Sutherland, 1990).

In literature this image is encapsulated by Tiny Tim in Dickens 'Christmas Carol', the saint like passive child grateful for the kind attentions of others. In the same category is the tragic figure of the Elephant Man who is paraded as an icon of pity. This is not the only image of the disabled, as common is the villain, the concept that deformity of body is matched by deformity of character. The list is almost endless: Dickens hunchback, Quilp; Shakespeare's 'Richard III'; the bad guys in 'Dick Tracy'; Captain Hook; the wheelchair confined Dr Strangelove; the villains in Ian Fleming's Bond novels; the deaf Little Bonaparte in 'Some Like it Hot'. Where are the heroes or even the ordinary citizen? The list is much shorter: 'A Man Called Ironside'; the deaf woman in 'Children of A Lesser God'. The portrayal of the autistic savant in 'Rain Man' is interesting because, with less than one per cent of autistic people so gifted, this presents another prevalent image, of the disabled person as possessing marvellous gifts or insights given, as it were, in compensation.

There are about six million disabled people in this country though numbers depend on definitions, where are their images on television as ordinary citizens, as members of neighbourhoods as seen in the soap operas or in fashion magazines for women? Are we unprepared for positive images of disabled women? The only role for disabled women in magazines is the slot traditionally known by the press as the T.O.T., the triumph over tragedy.

In the last few years much has been said of the importance of role models in stimulating work place achievement in under represented groups and even in producing solid citizens in the case of boys without fathers. Role models are, therefore important in setting out positive images. It isn't the case that positive images are lacking - everyone has heard of Stevie Wonder, Ray Charles, David Blunkett, Jack Ashley, the American wartime President Roosevelt, Beethoven... there are many examples of talented people who have enriched the world and who happen to be disabled. Why are these images not used to re-educate the able bodied?

All of these examples are male: to be a disabled woman is to be an invisible woman. Is this because disability and femininity are both associated with passivity, that both are less likely to be in employment, that a life bounded by the four walls of the home is seen as quite acceptable for women (Morris, 1989; Oliver, 1990; Lonsdale, 1990)? Disabled women are not even allowed the dubious role of villain, perhaps, because the active and aggressive life is consigned to men and not women.

While images and role models are important in challenging established ways of thinking, far more radical change are also needed if disabled people are to be valued members of society. The persistence of segregated education does not prepare disabled children for employment and independent life but socialises them into accepting a reduced role.

It was very limiting, the curriculum was very small and if you didn't want to do the work, no-one bothered to push you, it was up to you to motivate yourself... nobody ever seems to think that disabled people will achieve anything (Chapman quoted in Sutherland, 1990).

There are signs that change is coming: the repeated attempts to bring anti discrimination legislation to the statute book must surely be successful if only by the process of attrition; the criticisms of current thinking by various bodies such as the RTPI and the TUC. influence the way in which society views the disabled; the growth in literature on disability as a political issue; the increase in media attention to disability issues (The Disabling World series, Link, See Hear). All of these suggest a mood of optimism but much remains to be done. The final section examines the need for legislation in this country.

Anti discrimination legislation

Choices and rights - that's what we've got to fight for - Choices and rights in my life (Crescendo quoted in Sutherland, 1990).

Since 1982 there have no less than seven attempts to introduce legislation (Barnes, 1991) which would make unlawful discrimination against disabled persons bringing their situation in line with black citizens and women. Though each attempt has failed, sometimes through the shabby practice of 'talking out', there is increased support for each attempt and it seems likely that before long legislation will be enacted. Recognition by government would serve to highlight the basic rights of disabled people to work, to live independently, to receive a quality education.

The Americans with Disabilities Act, signed by President Bush in 1990, has been seen as a blueprint for the U.K. While it promises much it exhibits some of the same weakness as existing piecemeal British legislation. The Chronically Sick and Disabled Persons Act 1970 with its much maligned equal access as long as it is 'practicable and reasonable' is mirrored in the American 'provided this is readily achievable'. For the legislation to work disabled people will need to be active in taking the recalcitrant to court. It can be argued that Americans are much more speedy in taking legal action than their British counterparts which highlights that we need to ensure that, unlike the penalties associated with the Race Relations and Sex Discrimination Acts, there are real enforcement powers and severe financial penalties in any legislation framed.

29

It would be naive, of course, to suggest that legislation alone will create a world in which disabled people are given equal opportunities. The British experience reveals that the major impact is in the area of correcting individual behaviour, not in the more important changes to structures of disadvantage. Nevertheless, in the words of Colin Barnes (1991), himself a disabled person:

> The denial of equal rights for disabled people cannot be morally justified when other disadvantaged groups have protection under the law, no matter how inadequate that protection may be.

References

Barnes, C. (1991), *Disabled People in Britain and Discrimination*, Hurst, London.

Ilson, R. (1992), "Looking for the Words" in Barker, P.(ed) *Disabling World*, Channel 4 Television, London.

Lonsdale, S. (1990), *Women And Disability*, Macmillan, London.

Mason, M. (1992), quoted in Ilson, R. opus cit.

Morris, J. (1989), *Able Lives*, Womens Press, London.

Oliver, M. (1990), *The Politics of Disablement*, Macmillan, London.

Sachs, O. (1991), *Seeing Voices*, Picador, London.

Sutherland, A. (1990), *The Disabling Council*, Albany Films, Local Government Training Board.

Chapter 4

Ageism

It is as though walking down Shaftesbury Avenue as a fairly young man, I was suddenly kidnapped, rushed into a theatre and made to don the grey hair, the wrinkles and the other attributes of age and then wheeled on stage. Behind the appearance of age I am the same person, with the same thoughts, as when I was younger (Priestley in Puner, 1978: 7).

Images of age

Images are made not only from pictures but also from words. It is a number of years now since the more enlightened started to clean up their language in respect of race and gender. Phrases such as 'nigger brown' or 'nigger in the wood-pile' have been abandoned as offensive. Words such as 'blackmail' have been dropped in favour of the non colour based 'extortion'. The word 'chairman' has been abandoned and notions of a 'woman's place being in the home' provoke laughter but has this greater sensitivity extended to age? Elderly people are referred to in patronising terms ('old folks',' Derby and Joan', 'old biddy', 'old boy') or viciously with 'dirty old man', 'hag', 'old crone'. What about the term 'geriatric'- no one refers to children as pediatrics or women as whatever noun can be coined from gynaecology. Is it that elderly people are expected to be constantly at the doctor's or in need of hospitalisation, in other words perpetuating the myth of ill-health (Search, undated) and the concept that old age is a downhill journey to the grave.

Consider the images put forward by charities fundraising for the elderly. There is a similarity between the models they put forward and those used by charities for the disabled.

31

A poster of an unfortunate disabled child with a kind of heart rending caption on the end will quite clearly bring in more money than the poster of a stroppy disabled adult complaining to his local council about his lack of access (Oliver in Sutherland, 1991).

The elderly are also portrayed as objects of pity. In 1980 Help The Aged used the image of an elderly woman sitting in a chair, straining to look out of the window at the view beyond. The sky is blue conveying a bright summery day which this lady can only barely enjoy. The carpet is a square, not fitted, she wears socks and no stockings, the room looks bare. She is disabled and looks thin and undernourished. How is this to be interpreted? Because she is old she is cold, undernourished, poor, alone and dependent on others. An alternative view would be:

• She is poor because she has the lowest pension in Europe.

• Because she is poor she cannot afford to clothe herself properly - perhaps many of her purchases are from charity shops.

• Because she is poor she cannot afford to replace worn out furniture and effects.

• Because she is poor she cannot maintain her home.

• The complexity of the grant system and the lack of finance available to her local authority mean that she is not necessarily going to benefit from grant assistance.

• If it is supposed that she is a council tenant her local authority may have insufficient funds to adequately maintain her home or make improvements. The lack of available alternative housing may keep her fixed in the dwelling.

• She is isolated because she has poor access to transport.

• She has poor access to transport because transport policies and ideas about housing layouts mean that she has some distance to walk to a bus stop.

• She is transport poor because the vehicles are designed without thought of the elderly, disabled or parents with pushchairs.

• She is transport poor because it is not affordable.

• Because she is poor she has a limited choice of food made more limited by being restricted to local shops.

• Poor access to transport and out of town facilities based on the needs of car drivers limit her ability to reach the bigger shops which offer more choice and more competitive prices.

• Planning policies which have encouraged out of town shopping malls threaten the viability of her local shops.

• Because she is poor and because public utilities make a high charge for connection and demand large deposits, she has no telephone which increases her vulnerability and isolation.

• Because she is poor and not very mobile and her home is poorly insulated she has to economise on gas and electric consumption and is at risk from hypothermia.

• It ought to be borne in mind that old men and women can be black as well as white and that elderly black people are likely to be more isolated than their white peers. A study in Birmingham in the late eighties revealed that none of the thirty eight Asian women and fifteen from the forty-six Asian men who took part in the research were fluent in English (Cameron, Evers, Badger and Atkin, 1989). This issue will be discussed later in this chapter.

The poster invites the passer by to consider the miseries of old age and attribute them to old age not to social policy. No doubt this has the public diving into pockets and purses but what is the impact on the elderly seeing themselves portrayed as inevitably miserable and dependent? In the Birmingham research both black and white elders shared gloomy stereotypes of old age as a time of restricted outlook and activity, poorer health and mobility, and increased dependency (Cameron, Evers, Badger, and Atkin, 1989). The self perpetuating impact of negative images leads to a definition of ageism.

Exploring ageism

Ageism creates and fosters prejudices about the nature and experience of old age. These usually project unpleasant images of older people which subtly undermine their personal value and worth. Commonly held ideas restrict the social role and status of older people, structure their expectations of themselves, prevent them achieving their potential and deny them equal opportunities (Scrutton, 1990: 12).

Does ageism function in the same way as other areas of discrimination?. To begin with old age is not a club that an individual is born into unlike being black or being a woman. Old age is a club that we all want to join if only because it is better than the alternative in short those who survive will join it. Disability comes somewhere in between, being a club that we don't want to join, some have membership from birth and many others will have membership thrust upon them.

In other respects all four areas of discrimination are closely linked since they take as their basis the concept that biological difference and particularly visible signs of that difference mean that individuals with these 'signs' are different kinds of people and can justifiably be treated in a discriminatory fashion (Bytheway and Johnson, 1990).

One of the fearful developments in the consciousness of many old people is that, in the eyes of society, they have become another species. Ironically, an intensive caring and concern for their welfare is frequently more likely to suggest this relegation than indifference or neglect. The growing bureaucracy, amateur and professional, voluntary and state, for dealing with geriatrics, makes some old folk feel that they no longer quite belong to the human race any more (Blythe, 1979).

As with all areas of discrimination ageism has a three pronged form, not only fostering damaging images but also excluding individuals from various areas of life and thirdly oppressing individuals through violence.

Let us consider exclusion. The elderly frequently are given concessionary rates for evening classes which sounds beneficial though it can be argued that a bigger pension which allowed an elderly person to pay the full rate would be a more dignified model and one stripped of charity. These matters aside, educational bodies also frequently determine whether a class will run by the amount of fees raised not through numbers, so a class popular with elderly people needs to raise twice as many 'pupils' as any other and therefore has a greater chance of being dropped.

The most obvious example is employment. It isn't just that a man goes from being an employable 64 year old to being a retired non employable 65 year old though for many citizens this still holds true. For an increasing group, a loss of job in the mid forties is early retirement.

It is unlikely that anyone outside 35 - 45 years of age will have the necessary experience or drive essential for the rapid achievement required.

This advert is taken from *The Sunday Times* but any of the quality papers advertising 'top' jobs reveal the widespread use of age barriers. Conversely many local authority and housing association job adverts now contain an anti age clause:

FHA is committed to an equal opportunities policy and welcomes applications from all people regardless of their age, creed, disability, gender, race and sexuality (Inside Housing, 1992).

The chapter on 'Work' looks at this issue more closely and later in this chapter we'll return to consider ageism as discrimination which not only identifies a separate group but one which places a 'negative valuation [on] the ageing process throughout the life course' (Bytheway and Johnson, 1990: 33).

What of violence? It is a cosy thought that elderly people are treated with courtesy and kindness - that our ageism is patronising rather than pernicious - but one which does not stand up to much examination. An experiment by a nurse reveals, perhaps the real experiences of many older people:

Sheila Green, an 80 year old pensioner with poor hearing, dulled eyesight and shuffling gait, is treated rudely and dismissed as a second class citizen. But Sheila Green, the 38 year old nurse, is greeted politely - after she removes her disguise.

She wore a wig and dressed in clothes bought from charity shops. She put plugs in her ears to dull her hearing and drops in her eyes to impair her vision. With tape round her feet to make her shuffle, a brace on her back to make her stoop and restraints around her fingers to simulate arthritis, she went shopping, travelled on buses and attended a hospital out-patients department.

Describing her experiment in *Nursing Times* she said a bus driver told her "Take your bloody gloves off" as, in her pensioner role, she fumbled for her ticket. Without her disguise, she went through the same routine with the same driver. He waved her aside, winked at her and said "Sit down, love, I trust you" (Fletcher, 1991).

Steve Scrutton (1990) details how the physical abuse of elderly people in a private residential care setting was given scant media and social work attention. This compares with the headline making cases of Cleveland, of Rochdale and of abused children such as Maria Colwell. This differential attention can only spring from the view that children are the future while the elderly have had their life and are not so valuable.

It can be assumed that most Social Services departments have policies and procedures on child abuse though obviously the quality of these may vary considerably. How many have policies and procedures on 'granny bashing' - not such a well known but not an uncommon activity?

It is common for local authority residential care workers in homes for the elderly to be paid on manual grades while staff in children's homes are on APTC grades. Working with children is seen as having a responsibility for child development while work with the elderly is seen as unrewarding and largely about wiping bottoms

Another form of violence is the targeting of the elderly by the cutbacks being suffered by Social Services departments. In 1992 Newcastle MBC is making cuts in its revenue spending to avoid penalties from central government. Social Services is a high revenue spender and must bear a large slice of these cuts which in turn are disproportionately borne by the elderly. Children and young people are so protected by legislation, including the Children Act 1989, that services for them are untouched.

Consider the services that are on offer to elderly people by Social Services departments and Health services. Cameron et al assert that community care services 'fit' badly with the needs of older people and given that this is true, how more ineffective is the service likely to be in fitting the needs of black elderly people.

The inappropriateness of the response of the services to the needs of old or disabled black people was seen, however, in the provision of unacceptable aids, adaptations, often costly, that were not used because they did not meet cultural requirements, and bath nurses turned away, because their help with washing was interpreted as unhygienic (rinsing not being done in the customary way) or as an invasion of privacy (Cameron, Evers, Badger and Atkin, 1989: 245).

How many local Social Services authorities have meals on wheels which cater for vegetarians or those who eat halal meat? How many elderly people, entitled to a service find themselves excluded because the service does not take account of their needs but seeks to fit them into a white stereotype.

Concentrating on communication is only one small way of ensuring a greater take up of community services: issues of race cannot be reduced to matters of language. As with other services which will be discussed later in the book, making a change from an anglocentric service provision is more important than translating leaflets for minority groups for whom little provision is made.

Chronology

Earlier in the chapter we considered how ageism militates not only against the 'officially old' as it were but also against those who might consider themselves still to reach middle age. The example given was in job recruitment but this kind of ageism surrounds us. Next time you buy a birthday card have a look in the 'humorous cards section'. Lots of jokes about ripening not ageing, about the fire brigade standing by to put out the fire from the lighting of so many candles, comments about lessening sexual performance:

Between 20 and 30, if you feel OK, You can do it twice a day. From 30 to 40 if you're still alright, You cut it down to once a night. From 40 to 50 it's an occasional treat; From 50 to 60 it's an Olympic feat. From 60 on put your thoughts to bed, Just dream about it... For it's all in your head!!

For many people a birthday is not a cause of celebration but one for grieving particularly those birthdays with the nought at the end. Susan Sontag (1972) put it powerfully with:

People in industrial societies are haunted by numbers. They take an obsessional interest in keeping the score card of ageing, convinced that anything above a low total is some kind of bad news. In an era in which people actually live longer and longer, what amounts to the latter two thirds of everyone's life is overshadowed by a poignant sense of unremitting loss.

Much has been written about the double standard of ageing (most recently Germaine Greer in 1991). While both sexes have to suffer jibes about their loss of attractiveness or loss of sexual potency, the impact on women is more destructive. In spite of advances made by women, grey hair and wrinkles which might be seen as distinguished and signs of character on a man, cause a women to be treated with less attention. Try to think of older women who are promoted as attractive. They are all women who have managed by various means to look much younger (Joan Collins, Raquel Welch, Jane Fonda). Paul Newman with white hair and wrinkles is still viewed as a desirable man. Men are allowed to age, without penalty, in several ways that women are not. Perhaps the answer lies in society's construction of masculine and feminine. 'Masculine' is associated with competence, control and authority which may not be diminished by age. Indeed a middle aged man of fifty or more can increase his attractiveness through fame, power and money and at this age it is not uncommon for a powerful man 'to trade in' his wife for a younger model who gives him more kudos. Attributes of 'feminine' such as passivity, and noncompetitiveness, are not improved by age and woman's sexuality which is much more dependent on youthful beauty is more fragile.

The messages on beauty jars and hair colourants promise to keep age at bay and women are encouraged to begin these programmes early (in their twenties) if they want to keep turning heads.

However it is argued that society has created these double standards of ageing, in one important respect, chronology plays a more central point in a woman's life and that is in terms of fertility. The monthly period keeps women's eyes fixed to the calendar and the passage of time erodes and finally put an end to fertility which may be a cause of relief for some women but a great grief for others. Feminist writers, (Greer, 1991) themselves entering the menopausal years, are now focusing their thoughts on the post child-bearing years and refuting the notion that:

An old woman is for nature only a degraded being, because she is useless to it (quoted in Stearns, 1977: 32).

Legislation

In 1967 the United States Age Discrimination in Employment Act (ADEA) was passed to protect older workers from age based discrimination in recruitment, in promotion and access to training and to employee benefits. It is this kind of legislation which the British Campaign Against Age Discrimination in Employment (CAADE) would like to see implemented here. As chapters on other areas of discrimination have revealed legislation is not a panacea. Research undertaken in 1981 in the USA showed that little had changed in respect of older workers and that many employers had not even heard of the legislation much less considered their practices in relation to it (Pepper, 1982).

In Britain various campaigners have called for an 'ageless society':

In a speech to the British Association in August [Lord Darlington] called for an ageless society in which all information about people's dates of birth would be suppressed. Work would be spread more evenly through life and it would illegal to exclude anybody from a job simply because of age. This would eliminate the problem of an increasing dependent population of pensioners by accepting them as active individuals, people like everybody else (Appleyard, 1990).

The reality is that while unemployment for younger people, seen as more employable and in more need of a job, remains an unresolved political issue, age legislation is unlikely to make any headway. Nevertheless, restructuring of the economy warns that for some there may never be a job. One of the ways to combat this is to consider employment as a chapter in a person's life not practically the whole story. Such a society would need to radically alter its thoughts about retirement, the retired and older people.

References

Appleyard, B. (1990), "Playing on in extra time: how we moved the goalposts of life", *The Sunday Times*, 28th October, Section 3: 4.

Blythe, R. (1979), *The View in Winter*, Allen Laine, London.

Bytheway, B. and Johnson, J. (1990), "On defining ageism", *Critical Social Policy*, Autumn: 27-39.

Cameron, E.; Evers, H.; Badger, F. and Atkin, K. (1989), "Black Old Women, Disability and Health Carers" in (ed.) Jeffreys, M. *Growing Old in the 20th Century*, Routledge, London: 230-248.

Fletcher, D. (1991), "Not Disability But Discrimination", *Search*, November 11th: 15, Joseph Rowntree Foundation.

Greer, G. (1991), *The Change: Women, Ageing and the Menopause*, Hamish Hamilton, London.

Inside Housing, (1992), August 21st: 15.

Pepper, C. (1982), "Age Discrimination in Employment: A Growing Problem in America", Select Committee on Aging, House of Representatives, Washington D.C.

Priestley, J.B. quoted in Puner, M. (1978), *To The Good Long Life*, Macmillan, London.

Scrutton, S. (1990), "Ageism - The Foundation of Age Discrimination", in E. McEwen (ed.) *Age: The Unrecognised Discrimination*, Age Concern.

Search, undated, *Against Ageism*, Search, Newcastle upon Tyne.

Sontag, S. (1972), "The Double Standard of Ageing", *Saturday Review*, 23rd September: 29-38.

Stearns, P. (1977), *Old Age in European Society*, Croom Helm, London.

Sutherland, A. (1991), *The Disabling Council*, Local Government Training Board.

Section 2
Policy

Chapter 5

Planning for people

Introduction

> [planning] "regs" can become a check-list which defines the needs of disabled people ignoring, even disallowing, the possibility that individual professionals dealing with particular cases need to learn from the experience of disabled people themselves (Thomas, 1992: 25).

> I do firmly believe that the current generation of planners must break away from the view of the professional knowing best and demonstrate that planning can assist in improving the quality of people's lives. I'm not saying that this is easy; in fact it's complex, often frustrating, can bring conflicting views and is very time consuming. But I do believe its how we must proceed (McLoughlin, 1992).

These statements, one from an academic and the other from a practitioner, set the tone for this section on planning for people - all the people. Those readers looking for check-lists will be disappointed.

The needs of a particular community or a group within that cannot be reduced to a shopping list of policies. This mode of working suggests that the contact between these groups and their environment is confined to these points and that citizens from these groups need only be consulted on these particular matters

Race
- hot food take aways
- places of worship
- single sex recreation facilities
- house extensions

- slaughter houses
- burial grounds

Women
- safety issues in transport management
- child care / support
- location of shopping
- housing layouts

Disabled
- pedestrianization versus orange badge holders
- building design
- transport design and affordability
- recreation facilities

Elderly
- need for local shopping
- street furniture
- location of health facilities
- energy policies for low income users

It may also be based on a crude vision of society which fails to see that, for example, the black community is also made up of men and women, elderly men and women and disabled men and women.

It is not suggested that local planning authorities should abandon the idea of creating policies and guidance notes which are sensitive to different needs. It cannot be overstressed that these policies need to be developed as part of the broad strategy to overcome disadvantage within the planning process and not as ad hoc responses. Planning for all the people rests on talking to the community and more importantly listening and understanding what it is like to view the world from a particular outlook. In order to plan there is a need for understanding and respect. Out of dialogue policies may grow and be developed.

Many people in our society have considerable choice in their lives and with that comes choice about the way they use the immediate environment. People who have a car or ready access to a car have greater freedom of movement, the move to out of town retail sites gives more shopping choice to this group, they have readier access to green spaces. People who are in work, or rather some of those in work, and the better off among the retired have greater access to recreation and leisure opportunities many of which are dependent on ability to pay.

Inequalities are not simply created and sustained by income differences they derive from differences in opportunity. Women, black men and women, disabled men and women, gay men and lesbians, elderly men and women all suffer from discrimination in our society and cannot be said to enjoy equal opportunities. This discrimination may be direct, it may be as a result of lack of awareness on the part of policy makers or it may be in the form of harassment and violence.

Consider how the difficulties faced by these groups are made worse by the action of planners.

A move to favouring the private car over public transport leaves women who are less likely to be drivers or car owners without easy means of getting about. It presents similar problems for the elderly and those with mobility difficulties as well as children and teenagers who are robbed of independence. Poor design of the built environment and facilities restricts mobility for disabled people, for the elderly, for parents with young children. Restriction of mobility for the disabled can mean the difference between going out earning a living and having a full social life or being dependent and virtually housebound. Lack of attention to lighting and landscape maintenance can lead to women and elderly people self imposing a curfew after dusk. What about the safety needs of the black community? How confident are they about leaving their homes after dark, or indeed staying in their homes, given the problem of racial harassment?

Many of the problems faced by these groups of citizens are compounded by low incomes relating to economic policies, levels of benefits and discrimination in employment. Perhaps none of these are within the sphere of influence of planners, nevertheless land use policies can lead to the creation of employment opportunities for different groups. The encouragement of high level office work or research and development units offers employment to different groups from those given job opportunities by an encouragement of manufacturing industry. Urban regeneration policies based on gentrification or tenure change may cause a change of social composition leading to destabilising of local shops serving the original low income community. The closure of local shops because of the development of out of town shopping centres may lead to an elderly person losing independence and needing Social Services input to do her shopping for her. Griffiths (1989) sums up the position with:

> Modern cities have been criticised not just because they fail to provide adequate material *standards* of housing, transport, recreation, space and jobs... but also because they reproduce dominant power relations, so contributing in subtle ways to the oppression and exclusion of large sections of the population.

The briefest examination of any British town reveals the truth of this statement:

- the car speeds by while the pedestrian is asked to walk through dark tunnels - who drives and who walks?

- the creation of unsafe estates and night time town centres excludes women and the elderly from these spaces.

- the suburban housing estate geared to the car user constrains the more complex movements of women who have domestic duties as well as paid work.

- the built environment and transport system reveals the dominance of the able bodied over the disabled and the elderly.

43

What is planning?

In the last decade the debate has intensified as to what planning ought to be about. The Nuffield Inquiry in 1986 stated that there were two principles at the heart of planning: the first being that land is a unique resource and secondly that acceptable living conditions are secured through environmental controls. This is a point to which we'll return later. There is also the supposition that all development proposals need to be examined to determine whether they are in the public interest. Many planners have taken a people based, not a land based view, stating that planning is about creating and retaining communities with full access to a range of services and facilities necessary for maintaining a quality life for citizens. Hand in hand with this view goes the concept of planning acting as a redistributor of wealth, controlling land resources with an eye to need not to means or market demands for profits (MacEwen, 1991: 147).

During the Conservative era planning has been cast in the role of a facilitator of market forces, although since the mid eighties there has been some interest in a return to the more traditional regulatory role. Throughout this period, a major problem has been the relationship between development and social costs. Cast in the role of minimising the social costs that arise from development is not a role that all planners have found comfortable.

> Planning is in the same case as other public functions. The Planning system can contribute to the growth of equality or exacerbate differentials, planning is seldom neutral, and the attempt to define planning in purely technocratic terms, e.g. as the application of law to the regulation of land use, placed planners in a position of low esteem vis a vis the older profession (Eversley, 1990).

Some might question whether planning now has a role to play in reducing inequalities. The introduction of the Urban Programme in 1968 followed in successive years by other additional programmes - City Challenge being the latest - suggest that central government does not see mainstream planning as a useful vehicle for urban regeneration. The creation of additional programmes can be seen as a fundamental attack on the ability of planning to be involved in redistributing resources to the less well off (MacEwen 1991). The stripping away of community development issues firstly attempts to confine planning strictly to land use matters and secondly suggests that land use is not connected to the creation, maintenance or amelioration of disadvantage.

This is obviously incorrect, indeed this extract from *The Guardian* demonstrates the strong feeling that adherence to ideology in planning rather than knowledge of people has been to blame for many of our urban problems - in this instance the disturbances in Coventry in early 1992.

> The key issue in urban policy, however, is the problem of mono-functionalism, an ugly word for an ugly process. Coventry's Wood End and Willenhall estates were planned according to the strict zoning ideology of utilitarian modernism: rigid land use regimes separate work, housing and leisure into watertight compartments, connected only by the

car and a very occasional bus for the dispossessed... Not only has space been divided up with a mathematical rigour, time has been clearly segmented too. When the town centre is alive, the housing estates are dead (and vulnerable to burglary); when the shops close the town centre goes dark too (and becomes vulnerable to robbery and assault) (Worpole 1992: 21).

Many planners may comment as Robin Thompson (1990) did 'If we have such power to do harm, perhaps we also have the means to do good' .

The problem remains that planning is essentially reactive. The re-emergence of plan making as the basis for planning rather than a heavy reliance on development control is to be welcomed, nevertheless development anticipated in the plan may not take place. This is particularly true in the present climate with reliance on the market and the inability of the public sector to build or create infrastructure. Left to itself the private sector may choose not to respond and is likely to view investment in poorer or disadvantaged sections of the community as unprofitable.

While new development may be at a low ebb there is another role for the planner in assessing the differential impact of cuts on different needs groups in the community. The cut backs imposed by central government on local government has caused painful decisions to be made about the closure of leisure facilities and libraries. What is the effect of these closures on communities and on those groups who need local facilities for reasons of cost or safety and confidence? This surely is a role for planners.

Since inequality is part of the economic and social context of planning it is important that planners feel that they challenge dominant power relationships and work to ensure that the excluded are brought into the mainstream to enjoy a quality environment with quality services. Without keeping these objectives in sight planning is in:

> danger of playing exclusively to the needs and the interests of the upwardly mobile, the newly included, and the environmentally progressive yuppies at the expense of marginalised social groups (Mayer, 1991: 123).

While the government stance seems to be that planning is simply a regulatory function, there are a number of tools in the hands of planners. The next section examines the equal opportunities legislation in respect of planning.

The legislation

Disability

Central government has stated that, in spite of the existence of the Race Relations Act and the Sex Discrimination Act, both race issues and women's issues are not concerns for planners and planning, however disability issues are. Why the divergence? Perhaps because disability is seen by government as purely an issue of access and, therefore one which can be effectively tackled by planning authorities and building control. Access plainly is important and forms part of the third planning chapter but as the earlier discussion on discrimination against the disabled reveals there are deeper structural issues to be tackled. Central government has consistently refused to acknowledge this truth hence the lack of legislation on a par with the Race Relations Act and the Sex Discrimination Act.

While acknowledging the shallow view taken by central government, it must be said that through the pressure of the RTPI among other bodies, the position of planning in respect of disability has been strengthened from the initial weak position set out in Section 4 of the Chronically Sick and Disabled Persons Act (1970) and the Amendment Act (1976). This states that there should be provision for disabled people visiting public buildings and buildings where education takes place or which is a place of employment but only "in so far as it is practicable and reasonable".

Lobbying for enforcement powers failed but did result in an amendment (Section 29) being introduced to the Town and Planning Act (1971). This places a duty on planners to bring to the attention of developers of offices, shops, factories, railway premises and educational buildings the Chronically Sick and Disabled Persons Act 1970, the BSI Code of Practice BS 5810 1979 and more recently the Building Regulations 1985 Part M. The building regulation is the instrument by which the CSDP may be enforced though the requirement in the CSDP is weakly drawn.

In the field of development control there seems to be more progress with the Secretary of State taking a more robust line in Circular 10/82:

3.6 In addition, the provision of certain facilities for disabled people can raise planning issues which fall within the competence of local planning authorities. The arrangements for access to buildings can be a planning matter and the suitability of the arrangements for use by the public, which includes disabled people, raises issues of public amenity which, in the opinion of the Secretary of State, can be material to a planning application...

3.7... Where appropriate, conditions may be attached to a grant of planning permission to deal with the matter.

3.10 In the case of any appeals to the Secretary of State against the decisions of local planning authorities, it is his intention, where appropriate, to take due account of the considerations set out above in deciding whether to allow or dismiss the appeals or reverse or vary part of the decisions of local planning authorities or to decide the application as if made to him in the first instance (DOE 1982).

The 1985 Development Control Policy Note 16 Access for the Disabled restates the power of planners but also restates the constraints of the Chronically Sick and Disabled Persons Act 1970:

Resolving problems by negotiation will always be preferable, but where appropriate the planning authority may impose conditions requiring access provision for disabled people. Such conditions must be reasonable in all respects, relevant to planning purposes and enforceable. In considering conditions, local planning authorities will need to be mindful of their practicability both from a technical and an economic point of view.

While legislation is to be welcomed merely working to ensure strict compliance does not ensure easy access or improvement in opportunity for the disabled. Authorities are encouraged to make available to developers Access Guidance Notes which discuss the importance of thoughtful design in building interiors yet a failure to fulfil these requirements would not result in refusal of planning permission as the legislation stands at present.

Matters of internal design are deemed to be outside the control of planners thus it may be that a building conforms to building regulations but lack of thought or a desire to follow the letter not the spirit of the guidance prevents disabled people gaining any benefit from new provision.

It is important to consider that the building regulations and indeed the CSDP legislation covers only those who have problems in walking which is only a small group within the disabled community.

Race and gender

When examining the duties placed on planners in respect of race and gender we see that there are fewer requirements but that the failure to comply is unlawful: a very different ethos to that governing disability issues.

In addition to the general requirement placed on local government to act without discrimination and to foster harmonious race relations between communities there is a specific requirement on planning authorities set out in section 19a of the Race Relations Act 1976:

> it is unlawful for a planning authority to discriminate against a person in carrying out their planning function.

What does this mean? Plainly there is a requirement not to discriminate against a citizen on grounds of race or colour so that Mr Smith's planning application is accepted while Mr Patel's, under identical circumstances, is not. This will be discussed in the later chapter when consideration is given to ethnic monitoring, without which no planning authority can be certain that it does not discriminate.

As important is the more nebulous issue of indirect discrimination.

> Black people form distinct social groups, with their own group characteristics, attitudes and aspirations, and warrant close and specific scrutiny by town planners. Failure to do so represents discrimination against black people, since their particular circumstances will not be reflected in plans and policies will be prepared in ignorance of their problems and requirements... The false assumption by some that the values of town planning are transcendental must be challenged. Policies and decisions should reflect the values of the people affected; they should not be expected to conform to what is seen as normal or traditional by town planners or the planning system (RTPI / CRE, 1983: 24-25).

47

The planning response to indirect discrimination will be will be explored in depth in the second planning chapter which concentrates on planning for multi racial Britain.

The Sex Discrimination Act 1975 places a much weaker duty on planners though their activities could be said to be covered by section 29:

It is unlawful for any person concerned with the provision (for payment or not) of goods, facilities or services to the public or a section of the public to discriminate against a woman who seeks to obtain or use those goods, facilities or services-

(a) by refusing or deliberately omitting to provide her with any of them, or

(b) by refusing or deliberately omitting to provide her with goods, facilities or services of the like quality, in the like manner and on the like terms as are normal in his case in relation to male members of the public or (where she belongs to a section of the public) to male members of that section.

The following are examples of the facilities and services mentioned in subsection (1)

(e) facilities for entertainment, recreation or refreshment;

(f) facilities for transport or travel;

(g) the services of any profession or trade, or any local or other public authority.

Sheffield in its exploration of women's recreation needs put forward the following policy considerations:

• what is the level and type of involvement by women in recreation facilities?

• women have relatively lower incomes - does this affect their participation?

• residential needs of different groups of women e.g. black women, older women, young unemployed women, single parents.

• what is the role and nature of local / district facilities in women's involvement in recreational pursuits and activities?

• are existing recreation activities male dominated and does this affect women's involvement?

• can the plan provide recreation activities / facilities that enable and encourage women to participate?

• the design and management of recreation facilities e.g. access, child care, waiting and seating areas, cheap cafes, separate sessions and personal security is an important consideration in enabling women to enjoy recreational pursuits. How can the plan tackle these issues? (Sheffield City Council, 1989)

A sensitive authority should be mindful of the greater security problems facing women and consider these when formulating a transport strategy. Where should bus stops be positioned, should there be single sex services, can companies change to hail and ride service at night. The legislation talks of safe travel and this includes walking - an aware authority considering the refurbishment of an estate needs to take on board the experience of women in moving around their neighbourhood. These issues among others will be discussed in the third planning chapter, 'Planning for safety and access'.

Listening and learning

> One key to *achieving equality* is of course seeing people as consumers - as clients - as real - not simply as statistics; and a willingness to ensure that our policies, proposals and plans will really meet the needs of those clients. So the starting point has to be finding out about, understanding, and interpreting the needs of those clients (McLoughlin, 1992).

How many planners know the answers to the following questions in respect of the citizens of their town, city or district:

• how do non car owning elderly people access community facilities?

• how do parents with a pram and a toddler negotiate shop entrances?

• where do people with disabilities shop and how easy is it for them to get to them and use them?

• how do night shift and early shift workers complete their journey to and from work?

• how do women feel about living on some of the sixties built estates characterized by complex street patterns and high levels of planting?

• what is it like to use a pedestrian subway at dusk?

Many of our citizens face these demands and problems daily but to what extent are planners aware of their needs and therefore to what extent are their needs on the agenda?

Planning effectively for people is not simply about collecting knowledge; the LGTB truths speak to us as much about culture as strategies. Planning policies are implemented through planning agencies of one kind or another. each of these organisations has a culture of its own which will influence the plans, the planning policies and the ways that agency works. Griffiths and Amooquaye (1989) comment that town planning is not immune from the national political culture which empowers and sustains planning. Similarly attitudes to women and gender relations within the workplace will influence planners when considering the needs of women. The East Sussex Structure Plan (1975) talks about in migration but confines its remarks on women to commenting that they are attracted by the high quality housing and are largely indifferent to local employment opportunities. This sees women as non working appendages to employed men. Newcastle's Action Plan for women's issues (1987-1988) concludes that 'the most specific areas of relevance for women and planning' are the

49

design of shopping areas with regard to 'access for pram users and facilities for changing and feeding' and the 'range of shops' available. The Greater London Council was instrumental in providing specific plans for women to meet more effectively their specific needs, however, these two examples suggest that the focus is likely to be on women's needs that stem from their traditional gender roles (Davoudi, 1990 :26).

Effective working depends therefore on a recognition that, in defining key issues, planners may be bringing to bear a male world view (Sandercock and Forsyth, 1990) or one which is ignorant of the experiences of the black citizen. This recognition of personal limitation should be enough to get planners out into communities but planners also need to have a strong belief that the process of planning is as valuable as the end product. This should be second nature to planners since planning, unlike any other professional field, has consultation built into its processes. However, what may have evolved over time, in many authorities, is a minimalist approach in which as little as possible is being done to encourage participation and greater reliance is placed on the view of the professional. Making a change involves throwing away the out moded but comfortable view, 'An experienced officer has a good understanding of what the public wants'

> The officers seemed to have preconceived ideas on what comments to expect from the black community on issues, assuming there to be a homogeneous black voice, and seemed surprised when this did not occur... What came as a surprise to some officers was that the customers did not necessarily think the same way they do (duBoulay, 1989: 14).

Planners looking for a framework to begin changing their ways of working might consider the five self evident truths set out by the then Local Government Training Board (now Local Government Management Board):

- A local authority's activities are not carried out for its own sake, but to provide service for the public.

- A local authority will be judged by the quality of service provided within the resources available.

- The service provided is only of value if it is of value to those for whom it is provided.

- Those for whom services are provided are customers demanding high quality service and citizens entitled to receive it.

- Quality of service demands closeness to customers and citizens (LGTB, 1987: 4).

This citizen centred approach is not to be seen as a trend: a planning response to the customer charters and mini citizen charters that are springing up in the public and private sectors. If planning is about the management of spaces then planners need to know how people feel about that space. How do they use it? What changes does a space goes through in the 24 hour day - who uses it, when and for what?

Those who don't get involved are unlikely to see their needs identified, prioritised or resourced. How do we reach out to the community? To assume that groups of people are going to come rushing in when professionals announce that they have decided to stop ignoring them is to set situations up to fail. How easy it is to hold a public meeting and finding that few people turn up, say that it is because 'they' are not interested and don't want to be involved. The more likely answer is that those who have been ignored historically and are accustomed to finding barriers to their involvement are not likely to suddenly come forward to get involved in the usual consultation processes.

A local authority planner, when asked by one of my colleagues why no black and ethnic minority people had made comments on their draft UDP stated that "black people are not interested in planning". Yet no efforts had been made by the council to find out the exact reasons for non-involvement (Planning Aid for London, 1990: 6).

Planners need to work harder and take a more pro-active approach. The following thoughts are put forward by the London Boroughs Disability Resource Team (1991: 2):

• Making contact with and preferably visiting local groups of disabled people to establish communication channels, and ensuring that regular contact is maintained.

• Providing funding for specialist groups or specific meetings.

• Ensuring that there are local accessible meeting places where disabled people can meet to discuss issues of access and their environment.

• Making the authority's intention to promote full participation, access and integration well known in the local community.

• Using positive images of disabled people in all publicity.

• Ensuring that professionals have an understanding of the communication needs of deaf and hard-of-hearing people, and providing induction loops and sign language interpreters where necessary.

• Developing ways of genuinely involving disabled people's representatives in decision making and policy formulation processes.

These suggestions focus on planning and the disabled but are equally applicable to working with elderly people, with women and with members of the black communities. For example, women are often socialised into believing they have nothing of value to say. A sensitive planner will have this in mind and might choose to take a different style of meeting:

A feminist planner experienced in neighborhood consultation and participatory planning described her difficulties in trying to get people at public meetings to contribute on an equal basis... She responded, in one community, by asking people sitting in small groups at a large meeting to tell a story or anecdote about their neighborhood. People then had no trouble speaking out about their lives and their community. Previously silent or hesitant participants found that they too possessed knowledge. For example, women who were stuck in the suburb all day talked about the problems of public transport for themselves and their family. The format of storytelling proved accessible to a variety of people and gave courage for more involvement (Sarkissian, 1990).

Planners need to know where elderly people congregate such as lunch clubs and target them with letters offering to come and talk about the UDP or a planning proposal. Why not , with the cooperation of a sheltered housing scheme use their lounge facilities for a meeting with older people in the neighbourhood. Notices can be displayed in the post office, in the library, in the medical centre.

A judicious choice of publicity material and visual images can have the effect of stimulating interest from under-involved groups and encouraging their participation. The following example from Manchester illustrates this in respect of women.

The exhibition, "A Day in the Life", shows how planning impinges on the everyday lives of women. The display shows eight different women photographed in everyday situations, some of which cause them problems as their needs have not been considered in the planning process. The text is taken from interviews with the women themselves. For example, a black woman who is a lone parent is concerned about safety on the streets, especially after dark. An elderly disabled woman and her carer find access to public areas a problem. Issues covered include: shopping, working, home, transport, roads, security and leisure (Ritchie, 1990).

This concept could easily be used to give a platform to older people, or to black men and/or women or to men or women with disabilities.

The purpose of such activity is firstly to sensitize planners to the needs of the different groups in the community and secondly to bring people into the planning process and ensure that they define their own needs rather than have them defined for them. The increase in meaningful consultation should lead to a greater confidence in planners and planning. If carried out as participation as opposed to consultation this should lead to the inclusion of more people who can help make and implement policy.

References

Davoudi, S. (1990), *Women in the Workforce*, Working Paper No. 9. Department of Town and Country Planning, University of Newcastle upon Tyne, Newcastle.

Department of Environment (1982), Circular 10/82, HMSO, London.

Department of Environment: Welsh Office (1985), Development Control Policy Note 16, Access for the Disabled, HMSO, London.

duBoulay, D. (1989), "Involving Black People in Policy Formation", *Planning Practice and Research*, 1: 13-15.

Eversley, D. (1990), "Inequality at the Spatial Level" , *The Planner*, March 30th.

Griffiths, R. and Ammoquaye, E. (1989), "The Place of Race on the Town Planning Agenda", *Planning Practice and Research*, 1: 5-7.

Griffiths, R. (1989), "Beyond Welfarism: Environmental Quality, Town Planning and the Left" in proceedings of the conference *Planning Skills and the Core of planning Education*, Department of Planning and Landscape, University of Birmingham.

Local Government Training Board (1987), *Getting closer to the public*.

London Boroughs Disability Resource Team (1991), "A right, not a privilege", *Community Network*, Autumn, Vol 8 no.3:2.

MacEwen, M. (1991), *Housing, Race and Law: The British Experience*, Routledge, London.

McLoughlin, B. (1992), "Initiatives to Promote Quality and Equality through the Planning System", Proceedings of the conference Promoting Quality and Equality through the Planning System, March 26th, London.

Mayer, M. (1991), "Politics in the Post Fordist City", *Socialist Review*, January : 105-124.

Planning Aid for London (1990), "Losing the Planning Race", *WEB*, Autumn,no 15/16: 5-6.

Ritchie, S. (1990), "Women planning in Manchester", *WEB*, Autumn, no 15/16.

Royal Town Planning Institute (1988), Access for Disabled People, Planning Advice Note No 3, RTPI, London.

Sandercock, L. and Forsyth, A. (1990), *Gender: A New Agenda for Planning Theory*, Working Paper 521, Institute of Urban and Regional Development, University of California at Berkeley, California.

Sarkissian, W. (1990), Personal communication in Sandercock, L. and Forsyth, A. *Gender: A New Agenda for Planning Theory*, Working Paper 521, Institute of Urban and Regional Development, University of California at Berkeley, California.

Sheffield City Council, (1989), Sheffield UDP - Guide-lines on Disadvantaged groups and their needs. Client Sub-group, November.

Thomas, H. (1992), " Disability, Politics and the Built Environment", *Planning Practice and Research*, Spring, vol 7 (1), 22-25.

Thompson, R. (1990), "Planning for the Have-nots: believing in needs-based planning", *The Planner*, March 30th: 10-12.

Worpole, K. (1992), "Cities: the buzz and the burn", *The Guardian*, May 25th: 21.

Chapter 6

Planning for multi racial Britain

In all their professional activities, members shall seek to eliminate discrimination on the grounds of race, sex, creed and religion and in particular shall seek to promote equality of opportunity between people of different racial groups and good race relations (RTPI, 1984).

This code of conduct has been, supposedly, a statement of values held by RTPI members since 1984 and yet in 1988 the National Development Control Forum's review of good practice in relation to planning and race came to this uneasy conclusion:

... it is clear from some responses however, that in a minority of authorities covert racism underlies some of the objections received to planning applications from ethnic minorities and possibly some of the decisions (NCDF, 1988).

In the previous 'Planning for People' chapter the emphasis was on communication and building awareness of needs and aspirations. This chapter examines ways in which planners may use their knowledge to eliminate racism. This first section examines the use of ethnic monitoring and draws on the research of Frank Riley, who undertook a questionnaire survey of 65 authorities in 1991 in respect of equal opportunities policies and ethnic monitoring of planning applications. The second section examines some examples of how local authorities are incorporating black needs into the plans and policies and explores the reasons why many planning authorities are not taking action.

Being seen to be fair: using ethnic monitoring

> In order to inform their assessment of their policies and practice to see if discrimination is occurring, local authorities should ensure that valid information is collected on racial groups... Local planning authorities should monitor the impact of their policies on racial minorities (RTPI / CRE, 1983).

The chapter on 'Racism' looked at ethnic monitoring from the perspective of denial of British citizenship: from another perspective it is only through rigourous and universal ethnic monitoring and analysis of the same that black people can be sure that their rights of citizenship are being respected.

The quotation, from the 1983 report made it quite clear that planning authorities have a need to monitor their decisions yet a survey undertaken by Frank Riley in 1991 of fifty six planning authorities (many with significant black communities) revealed only 16 who were monitoring race equality aspects of planning policies. Riley's study charts the progress of four local authorities, Leicester, Leeds, Sheffield and Newham LBC, with the highest levels of data collection on ethnicity of applicants. Leicester and Leeds began by using officer classification by applicants name which does yield data about the Asian community but which gives a nil response in terms of Caribbean peoples who may be named Moira Stuart or Trevor Macdonald.

In recognition of the crudeness of their methods, Leeds who were using monitoring as a means of finding out about black needs identified Chapeltown as an area of Afro-Caribbean concentration. The applications from that area were analysed. This revealed that only one application could be attributed to the black community and therefore Leeds took a closer look and focused on particular communities within the Chapeltown area.

> The Khoja community's use of a residential property in the Beeston Road was initially unauthorised. Soon after complaints were received from neighbours, who's major source of complaint arose from an annual September religious festival which lasts for 12 days and involves night time activity. Enforcement action was authorised by members. The community claimed that they had been unfairly treated by the planning authorities and were more likely to be refused planning consent than the rest of the communities. However, since there was no direct evidence of "racial motivation" ... the accusation could not be substantiated and the allegation was withdrawn. A planning application seeking to regularise the use was refused in October 1984 on traffic and amenity grounds. The appeal heard a year later, was rejected by the inspector. The applicants were given six months to relocate and the inspector asked the planning authority to give appropriate assistance in finding an alternative location for the Muslim Centre. Several factors arose from this case worthy of note. Firstly the Khoja community did not consult the planning department before purchasing the freehold of the property and so have committed themselves to a significant investment. As a result of these findings the following points were noted:

55

- the importance of early contact with minority communities where a requirement for premises is identified.

- the lack of a corporate system for identifying sites and premises.

- the need for consultations with black communities to identify other future communities needs and aspirations and to explain how the planning service can help.

- the need to consider providing guide-lines for the location of places of worship and associated activities (Riley, 1991: 58).

The studies of Leicester and Leeds indicate that initial attempts at monitoring reveal that Asian applicants were more likely to be refused planning consent than White applicants. Although, much of the initial refusal rate disparities were [later] explained by causal factors such as application type:

> One could imagine the concern caused by the City Planning officer's original analysis which could only explain 20% of the refusal rate variance between Asian and white applicants. How many put the unexplained 80% down to racial or ethnic discrimination and how many applications from Asians were treated more favourably as a result (Riley, 1991: 43).

Subsequent changes to services and, in some, cases policies, have corresponded with reduction in the disparity of refusal rates. Some of the reduction may well be attributable to the changing nature of planning applications by Asian communities that is fewer applications for hot food take aways which are always problematic in terms of increased traffic and possible nuisance from noise and fumes. Many planning authorities have restrictions confining these uses to shopping areas while others refuse change of use from shops (A1) to take aways (A3). These issues will be discussed later in the chapter.

If racism is part of the picture then, as Riley suggests, the process of monitoring may in itself inhibit its influence on the decision making process in development control.

Given the need to develop customer care strategies which must plainly include all the customers there is a need for all planning authorities to address the question of ethnic monitoring, not simply of planning but all services. This should be used not just as a means of testing who gets what but also of identifying unmet needs on the part of customers. This demands political will and planning is, of course, a political process. The particular path taken by each of the four case study authorities examined by Riley is undoubtedly influenced by the wider political context, in particular the amount of pressure for change which the black communities can bring to bear upon the authority. Leicester can rely on its greater numbers (25+ per cent) and political influence exerted by the black communities to support its pioneering attitude to monitoring and its up front approach to development issues. In Leeds, the leader of the council committed the authority to tackle racial discrimination through specifically targeted equality programmes. Riley suggests that the relatively small black population with its, therefore, fairly weak political clout has led to a reluctance by the Planning department to admit the need for more radical changes to policy highlighted by the monitoring thus confining it to service changes. Sheffield, by way of contrast, has a small black population but its work demonstrates commitment to creating improved opportunities for black Sheffielders.

Policy responses

Struggling for the answer

Following the revelations made by Leicester in 1981 that planning applications by members of ethnic minority groups were more likely to fail than those submitted by white applicants, some planning authorities took action. But what kind of action? It is clear that for many planners the Leicester study showed that they (the black communities) had problems. Planners and applicants were unable to communicate well because they did not have sufficient grasp of English. Planning applications failed because they had no notion of planning legislation. The solutions posed were often of a cosmetic kind; the translation of guidance leaflets, the introduction of black workers through section 11 with the intention of educating the black communities about the planning system. This sounds jaundiced: it is not that these are poor responses to the issues but that the problems don't lie with them alone.

Nor is the problem simply one of direct racism causing applications from black people to be judged less favourably. The stumbling block to equality is that the planning system and the general approach of planners is Anglocentric and to an extent mirrors a Britain of the 1940s and 1950s.

Central to the argument was an assumption that the problem centred on cultural misunderstanding which could be rectified by increasing the sensitivity of planners to ethnic differences, bringing the provisions of the 1976 Race Relations Act to their attention, and encouraging black communities to participate in an essentially unreconstructed planning system (Griffith and Ammoquaye, 1989).

This issue continues to cause great anxiety to planners. Part of the concern has been the clinging to the 'colour-blind is best' attitude in spite of the RTPI / CRE (1983: 15) emphasis that uniform treatment invariably has unequal outcomes for black citizens.

Another source of pain is what might be summarised by the phrase 'we town planners have a duty to safeguard the environment for future generations which means that we must protect people from their own excesses or lack of awareness of the consequences of their desires'. Against such thinking must be set the view that cities actually belong to their people and not to the planners. Given the widespread adherence to the former, the latter, no doubt, smacks of heresy.

When looking at the needs of the black communities within our cities, planners seem to cast themselves in a dilemma over the issue of whether the needs of the black community are converging with the white.

To what extent will the policies of the Plan affect the settlement pattern of the black population and contribute to its segregation or dispersal? For example, policies on housing; employment, shopping etc. will all have some implications on where people decide to live (Sheffield City Council, 1989: 6.58).

If the reverse decision is taken, that is not to invest in 'black areas' or to recognise diversity, will this encourage dispersal and is dispersal therefore the preferred choice to concentration? It is worth taking a little time to disentangle this argument. Sheffield has discovered that the Afro-Caribbean population of its city is dispersing, while the Asian communities are concentrating. These issues are explained to a degree by the younger nature of the Asian population and therefore the greater likelihood of living in a family with children and family re-unification of Bangladeshis. Other factors include stricter cultural imperatives on the lives of Asian people whose dietary needs are served by specialist shops such as Halal butchers and whose places of worship play a larger role in the community than Christian churches.

A survey conducted in Leicester in 1985 revealed that 60 per cent of Asian origin citizens did not want to move from their present home while of the remainder 63 per cent wanted to stay in the inner city. The reasons they gave for their preference were family and community ties, the availability of places of worship and specialist shopping facilities (Farnsworth, 1989). Plainly the policies of Leicester have contributed to catering successfully to the needs of the community which is part of the planning role. Having said that there is a need for all local planning authorities to establish the aspirations of their black communities and the reasons for their present location. Are black citizens concentrated out of preference or does clustering to combat racial harassment figure largely in location choice if choice is the word. What part does unemployment play in fixing families to a locality. What is the role of housing availability and affordability in preventing movement or increasing the decline of extended families against the preferences of the families in question? None of these should prevent planners responding to area based needs of black communities but should alert them that the encouragement of certain employment bases or of housing of particular types in other localities might present new opportunities for some citizens from the black communities. Needless to say the selection of other localities should be done in consultation with the black communities (Forman, 1989).

Another element of planners anxiety is the concept that a mixed use environment is not as desirable as a mono functional approach to planning. Robert Farnsworth comments that this springs from an Anglo-centric view and a failure to see that other groups may view the world differently:

> A mixed use environment which provides for all needs locally inevitably brings shared negative externalities alongside collective benefits and an intense sense of place. The existence of a cultural preference for this... rather than desire for an individual environment minimising spillovers, indicates that the long term organisation of the planning system itself involves a bias against many black lifestyles.

Does mixed use inevitably result in a second rate environment? Certainly if shops and businesses are going to be located very close to or within housing areas then the planner's role of ensuring that buildings look good and function properly is even more important. If residents are going to have a closer relationship with a building then planners need to ensure that it fits into the street scene.

Think about striking out the references to the black community and substituting women or people with disabilities, for example this statement from Leicester's Draft Local Plan:

> The extent to which women return to the workforce will depend on a number of factors amongst which... ease of access to a job will be important. The Draft Local Plan addresses this latter issue and considers how the location of employment, particularly within service industries, can affect the successful tapping of the pool of female labour currently remaining within the home. The problem of accessibility applies equally to disabled people who would benefit from jobs near their homes (1990: 29).

Leicester propose that locating sources of employment near to or within residential areas would help eradicate some of the disadvantage suffered by these two under-employed groups. No one presumably considers this to be controversial. Don't women also need to have community facilities near their homes in recognition of their security needs? What is the problem with taking the same attitudes to the black communities? Is it that as the RTPI / CRE said (1983: 15):

> Race is a sensitive subject because racists have made it so. The fears of intelligent and rational people to raise the issues in public represent one of the most important victories for those who promote racial hatred.

While many planners are uneasy of the possibilities and legalities of positive action it would seem that planners are uniquely placed to redress the inequalities suffered by black citizens.

> The oppression of "race" is, in fact, one which has particular relevance for town planners because of the fact that the racial structuring of social life has a very marked locality aspect. The operation of discrimination in housing and job markets coupled with the need for mutual support within ethnic communities faced with a dominant culture that is hostile and racist, has led to distinct areas of black settlement. British town planners, for their part, have a tradition of area-based ways of working. Indeed, for many planners, their "locality orientation" - their concern to try to deal in a comprehensive way with the characteristics and needs of individual localities - is a key element of their collective professional identity, setting them apart from their fellow local government professionals who are mainly concerned with the delivery of *services* rather than the management of *places* (Griffiths and Amooquaye, 1989: 5).

Few planners would disagree with this statement and yet there is little action being taken. Is another part of the problem the lack of guidance from central government? The preceding chapter recalls Christopher Chope's publicly stated view that race was not an issue for planners and certainly a planner looking for guidance in the Planning Policy Guidance Notes finds only a brief mention in PPG 12 (February 1992):

The Regulations also require planning authorities to have regard to social considerations in preparing their general policies and proposals in structure plans and UDP part 1s. But, in preparing detailed plans too, authorities will wish to consider the relationship of planning policies and proposals to social needs and problems, including their likely impact on different groups in the population, such as ethnic minorities, religious groups, elderly and disabled people, single parent families, students, and disadvantaged and deprived people in inner urban areas.

This statement has been developed out of PPG 15 and from DoE circular 22/84 both of which confine their attention to black people and the elderly. The considerable pressure placed on central government has raised the profile of disability issues and planning and yet on race there is continued silence on how planners may respond to our multi racial , multi cultural society. The recommendation for a Development Control Policy Note was made in 1983 (RTPI / CRE) but is still awaited. What is needed is a concerted campaign by planning authorities and the professional bodies to press for guidance from the DoE. Perhaps now is an appropriate time to begin that campaign since the results of census will soon be available which will give weight to calls for greater justice in the planning process. Planners need to have the support of central government if they are not to see their aims being overturned; for example a number of authorities have instituted (Haringey) or considered (Leicester) policies of relaxed development control standards within spatially defined boundaries to cater for the needs of extended Asian families. These policies have been challenged by the Secretary of State who will not grant that race might be a material consideration. Other authorities have used personal planning permissions though, again, the wording of PPG 1 suggests that such use is not encouraged.

Unless otherwise specified, a planning permission runs with the land and it is seldom desirable to provide for any other arrangement. Exceptionally, however, the personal circumstances of an occupier, personal hardship, or the difficulties of businesses which are of value to the character of the local community, may be material to the consideration of a planning application. Such arguments will seldom outweigh the planning considerations. If the proposed development entails works of a permanent nature they will remain long after the personal circumstances of the applicant have ceased to be material.

Again this clause might be altered to take account of cultural imperatives.

Playing the numbers game

It has been argued to a wearying degree that positive action is inappropriate for all but those local planning authorities with substantial black populations such as the Leicester's of this world. Leicester will be discussed later but it is worth reflecting that our concepts of British towns and cities and, for that matter, countryside are often far from the truth. James Derounian in a forthcoming examination of rural Britain quotes from the recent CRE research on the south west. The general view of these areas is that they are 'white': the research reveals around 32,600 black citizens in Cornwall, Devon, Somerset and Dorset.

A recent survey undertaken by the CRE of local authority environmental health officers shows a widespread startling lack of knowledge on the population served (Ratcliffe 1992). This is sobering for those who state that the coming of the census will be a revelation and from knowledge will spring action. Yes the census asked 'ethnicity' questions for the first time but shouldn't local authorities have knowledge of their customers if they are to provide services oriented to needs?

Some authorities have better knowledge bases to work from but the percentage of the black population calls forth very different responses.

Newcastle with a black population of four percent issued its draft Unitary Development Plan in May 1991. In the appendices to the plan Newcastle makes the following statements:

Equal opportunities: The City Council is concerned that all its activities should be undertaken within an equal opportunities context. In applying the policies and proposals of the UDP the City Council will consider the needs of relatively disadvantaged people. Every effort will be made to ensure that these needs are addressed in order to reduce social deprivation and polarisation.

Race equality: The City Council welcomes the fact that Newcastle is a multi racial City and is determined to ensure that all people feel at home. There are barriers to achieving this objective, and the City Council will do all in its powers to overcome them. All sections of the community have an equal right to the maintenance of their distinctive identities and loyalties of culture, language and religious custom. As a provider of community and personal services the City Council will take steps to ensure that these services are provided to all who need help.

An examination of the UDP reveals few mentions of the black community and specific policies seem to exist only in relation to the need for larger houses to meet the needs of extended families whose income levels are often low (Newcastle Draft UDP Sections 2.177 - 2.179).

This can be contrasted sharply with Sheffield's UDP. Sheffield, with a black population of about 4.5 per cent, has taken a citizen centred approach to planning their city in contrast to the traditional land based approach. This was prefaced by the document 'The UDP: What's in it for me?' published in November 1989 which examined in turn the needs of the following seven groups: the elderly, young people, women, people with disabilities, people living in poverty, the black communities and travellers. While not necessarily providing answers or proffering possible policy avenues this document is stimulating in that it continually poses questions and asks how the plan for Sheffield and the policies that result can meet the different needs identified. In short it establishes an ethos of change. The document's general statements likewise speak of commitment to anti racism and the relevance of these concerns for planning.

The importance of addressing issues of racism / racial discrimination and promoting equal opportunities within the UDP. cannot therefore be over-emphasised. These guide-lines will hopefully start the process (Sheffield City Council, 1989).

Using planning policies to promote race equality

Town planning is all about fulfilling people's needs. By recognising that different communities within our society have different cultures, values and aspirations this Plan can help to reflect these needs and by implementing its policies and proposals in a positive way the City Council can contribute to the elimination of racial discrimination, the promotion of equality of opportunity and the improvement of race relations for the benefit of all (City of Nottingham, 1988:177).

This section considers some of the ways in which local planning authorities have worked to meet the needs of the black community. At the risk of repetition the reader is warned not to take these policies out of context but to consider them as possible options to be discussed with the black community.

Shops and retailing

Sheffield City in its 1989 documentation guide-lines for the UDP discusses the shopping needs of black Sheffielders. While the black population lives in a number of districts five shopping centres have become centres catering specifically for their everyday shopping needs such as food though one or two services such as travel agents have also appeared. In discussing shopping needs, the plan draws attention to the low car ownership among the black communities which combined with low income means that shopping centres have to be within walking distance of home. Retailing provides few job opportunities but does give opportunities for black citizens to start their own business thus finding a way out of benefit dependency and discrimination in the job market. In Sheffield, as in other cities, the concept of the black entrepreneur is exposed a something of a myth since many shops and businesses exist at the margins of profitability serving a poor community. Low turnover can make it impossible for owners to invest in the property resulting in a shabby and unwelcoming appearance.

Sheffield goes on to pose a number of questions some of which are replicated below and used as a framework to highlight examples of practice and policies which address these issues:

- Do local corner shops need special protection in view of their importance to black communities especially within or near to Areas of Poverty? Are there enough corner shops in the right location?

While a large proportion of the population has gained from increased retailing efficiency and a wider range of choice, a significant proportion, including the poor and less mobile, has suffered from the reduction of convenient local shopping facilities. The economics of modern retailing has resulted in a pattern of fewer and larger shops... Planning permission will normally be granted for additional local convenience shops in areas which are considered by the City Council to be deficient in local shopping facilities, provided that the gross floorspace of any development does not exceed that necessary to overcome the deficiency (City of Nottingham, 1988: 54-55).

- There is likely to be increasing demand for comparison goods shops catering for black communities. What role is there for the Plan in facilitating and encouraging this?

- There may be demands for certain services e.g. travel agents; banks; estate agents; solicitors (offices generally); what particular policies (including positive action policies) are necessary to ensure that the provision of such services is not frustrated by restrictive planning policies.

Lambeth Borough Council has a policy which resists change of use from retail to non retail on ground floors in main shopping frontages however an exception is made where the proposed non-retail use would aid the development of black businesses; or provide services of particular benefit to black customers where it is desirable to be located in a main shopping frontage. The type of use includes a building society or some financial institution (Lambeth, LBC 1983).

Nottingham makes a presumption in favour of extensions to shops, even where they are not situated within defined shopping centres. The City Council has attempted to ensure that the expansion of local retail businesses (many are owned and operated by Asians) is made possible under certain circumstances (City of Nottingham 1988, Policy S. 14).

- Is there a need for targeted area improvement to enhance certain shops and shopping centres.

Nottingham City have introduced a "Brighter Shops" campaign which gives financial assistance to owners who want to make improvements. Grants are given to help owners renovate their shop frontages including upper floors. These have been targeted at areas with concentrations of poorer citizens who need local shopping because of lack of mobility and income. (City of Nottingham 1988:63).

Employment

To an extent these issues are related to the discussion of shops and retailing since, for many black citizens self employment is one of the few routes to employment. Sheffield (1989: 6.43) cites community representatives who talk of up to 90% unemployment in their particular community. The extent of unemployment in the black community is such that self employment cannot be the answer for all.

- Black people have been and continue to be in a severely disadvantaged economic position; what can the plan do to address this?

• Should we take account of the location of black people in identifying land for employment opportunities in order to create employment opportunities for this population?

Given the size of a local authority's work force and spending power there is an opportunity to lead by example.

Coventry City Council (1990) states in the UDP that:

The City Council will encourage employers to adopt equal opportunities guide-lines in their employment conditions. The City Council will monitor its own employment practices to ensure that they set a good example (E.5).

Leicester adds that employers should facilitate the employment of under-employed groups by providing child care and by:

ensuring that employment opportunities are located in areas which can be made accessible by forms of transport which are available to disadvantaged people (Leicester, 1989: E 12).

• To what extent can section 52 agreements be used to promote opportunities in employment for black people.

The City Council is keen to discuss and if necessary draw up voluntary agreements about any schemes to improve the accessibility of disadvantaged groups to jobs (Leicester, 1990: E 12).

• There is a need for more skills training facilities, taking into account the needs of different sections of the black community e.g women, young people, etc. These need to be easily accessible to black people e.g. near to black populations.

Newcastle MBC was one of the eleven local authorities who was successful in the first bidding round of City Challenge in 1991. The City Challenge area is the West End; an area of poverty and poor reputation (even before the disturbances of September 1991) with a significant Asian population. Much of the challenge programme is geared to creating routes back into the mainstream economy through the creation of training places, child care places and more community support. Specific ventures for the black communities include the establishment of a Black Women's Enterprise Centre. However, while these special ventures are welcomed, it is as important that the black population benefits from the whole package of training proposals in short that opportunities are not lost to eradicate barriers to employment. Those setting up training schemes, those working in job centres and careers advisers need guidance on operating equal opportunities. Issues of this nature are explored in the chapter on 'Work'.

Community facilities

Sheffield comments on community facilities does not confine itself to asking about provision of places of worship but also addresses the question of the under-participation of black people in sport and recreation and suggests that facilities may become intimidating and even 'no-go' areas if action is not taken. The answer may lie in a further question that Sheffield asks about targeting and using positive images of black athletes and sportsmen and women. Certainly the encouragement of women only sessions must help though again the first step must be to find out what activities the black population might enjoy.

- What other issues need to be addressed in promoting greater participation by women. To what extent do dogs in local parks discourage some women and their children from using them?

Leicester sets out the following requirements in respect of play spaces: The location, siting and design of play spaces must take account of the need to provide safe access, road safety, supervision, and the need to avoid nuisance to residents. Provision must take into account the needs of children of different ages, girls and ethnic minorities and children with disabilities. Play spaces should be capable of being fenced to make them secure against dogs (Leicester, 1990: R 10).

- Is there a need for flexible planning policies to allow the use of a house for a drop in centre for black elderly in certain areas.

The City Council will generally consider favourably the development (including change of use) of social, cultural or community uses... buildings within a residential street where the building will primarily serve the local community and the capacity of the building is less than 30 people (Leicester, 1990: LF1).

A frequently raised issue is the demand for places of worship. Leicester City comments that such facilities need to be located close to communities particularly where car ownership is low or religious beliefs require prayers to be made daily or more frequently. Leicester is disposed to giving planning permission for change of use to a place of worship but has a lengthy number of conditions which must be met particularly in the case of a residential street. Coventry states that the conversion of residential property will generally not be acceptable:

except where there is overwhelming need and expressed demand for a facility and no other suitable site or property is available in the vicinity (Coventry, 1990: 129).

Conclusion

This chapter has examined the anxieties and some of the achievements of planners in addressing their role in promoting a multi cultural Britain which recognises and values its many communities. The goal is not simply creating policies for their special (or more honestly, unmet) needs but recognising the black communities as citizens:

A step forward is the inclusion of black groups in the consultation process of the Unitary Development Plan. Their inclusion is based not only on them being black, but on the recognition that, in their own right, they are the main contact on groups on specific issues. For black people this means they are beginning to be treated as people who can contribute to planning issues as users of services and not just as ethnic minorities who happen to be disaffected by the process (duBoulay, 1989: 14).

References

City of Coventry, (1990), Draft Unitary Development Plan, May.

Department of the Environment (1992), Development Plans and Regional Planning Guidance, Planning Policy Guidance 12, February.

Department of the Environment (1992), General Policy and Principles, Planning Policy Guidance 1, March.

Derounian, James (forthcoming), *Another Country*, Bedford Square Press.

duBoulay, D. (1989), "Involving Black People in Policy Formation", *Planning Practice and Research*, 1:13-15.

Farnsworth, R. (1989), "Urban Planning for Ethnic Minority Groups: A Review of initiatives taken by Leicester City Council", *Planning Practice and Research*, 1: 16-22.

Forman, C. (1989), *Spitalfields - a battle for land*, Hilary Shipman, London.

Griffiths, R. and Ammoquaye, E. (1989), "The Place of Race on the Town Planning Agenda", *Planning Practice and Research*, 1: 5-7.

Lambeth LBC, (1988), Draft Brixton Town Centre Action Area Plan.

Leicester City Planning Department, (1990), "Leicester 2001: Draft Local Plan".

National Development Control Forum (1988), Unpublished report.

Nottingham City Council, (1988), Local Plan, Written Statement, August.

Newcastle MBC, (1991), Unitary Development Plan, Newcastle upon Tyne.

Ratcliffe, P. (1992), Personal Communication.

Riley, F. (1991), *Monitoring Race Awareness in Planning*, unpublished dissertation, Department of Town and Country Planning, University of Newcastle upon Tyne.

Royal Town Planning Institute / Commission For Racial Equality, (1983), *Planning for Multi Racial Britain*, CRE, London.

Sheffield City Council, (1989), "Ethnic Minorities", Sheffield UDP - Guide-lines on Disadvantaged Groups and their Needs, Client Sub-Group, Sheffield.

Chapter 7

Planning for safety and access

This chapter considers two issues: getting about in safety and getting about at all - how poor design creates barriers to free movement.

Security: getting about in safety

Living with the fear of crime

Every city has at least one estate where the quality of housing is poor

- an estate where the layout is confusing and complex.

- an estate with 133 per cent car parking - a standard dating back from the days when the car owning democracy was imminently expected - great tarmac areas now abandoned to children's ball games if they can dodge the broken glass.

- green buffer spaces where litter collects in bushes and where muggers are feared to find hiding places.

- walls where new graffiti covers old.

- broken street lights.

What messages do these places convey? Research done at both ends of the 1980s (Lewis and Maxwell, 1980; Skogan, 1987) demonstrate that physical deterioration combined with anti social behaviour such as verbal abuse, noisy neighbours or simply groups of youths hanging around the street corner can generate fear. These combined factors signal that here is a place that is out of control lived in by aggressive people who don't consider themselves bound by social controls (Painter, 1992). What might it be like to live in an area in such decline? Quotes from interviewers undertaking a household survey in the West End of Newcastle provide some insights into these feelings:

People are frightened to go out and won't go to facilities. Fear is for personal safety and burglary to their homes when empty.

The elderly are terrified, especially at night.

Crime generally, the people are really frightened. They all know someone who has been the victim of crime, but no one themselves had been victims in the last six months. it is the fear of crime which predominates. Dusk time is the most frightening for people .

People felt safe during the day but at night there was fear of attack (Newcastle City Action Team, 1992).

Fear limits where an individual may go, when they can go, how they can go and with whom they can go. Consider the messages (literally) conveyed to certain groups. How does it feel to walk through areas of racist graffiti? It is comforting to know that most racial harassment takes the form of written or verbal abuse rather than violence but it is also worth remembering that the person who coined the adage 'sticks and stones may break my bones but words can never hurt me' was not representative of human kind. It is natural that the person who sees 'Kill all Pakis' chalked on the wall may fear that perpetrators may, one day, prefer action to words. A society which turns an indifferent eye to graffiti may not care when your windows are broken or your children beaten up. Research undertaken by the CRE (1987) and the DoE (1989) reveals that there is a correlation between levels of graffiti and more serious acts of harassment. What is needed is a package of measures to tackle the fear. Some elements of the package are simple matters of good maintenance:

- regular inspection of street lights.

- skips left on a regular basis to ensure that bulky rubbish is not dumped to create an eyesore and health hazard.

- regular pruning of shrub planting.

- dog warden schemes to round up strays.

- street cleaning.

- graffiti squads to deal with racist and other offensive daubs.

Writing a shopping list is easy but it is also too easy to dismiss the possibility of improvement by stating that there is too much pressure on the revenue budget. This is not to underestimate the revenue problems faced by local government but it is worth considering the problem from another view point. In some of the unpopular estates there are maintenance problems but it is not that road sweeping or landscape maintenance don't happen they just aren't done well. Is the root of this problem financial or is it that some estates and their residents are considered to be less equal, less deserving of a good service. Increasing the frequency of services may be difficult or impossible but ensuring a standard of quality is a controllable issue. The ways into this are also well known but are dependent as much on a culture change within the organisation as new ideas for involvement:

- household surveys

- setting up quality circles that is groups of residents to give feedback on services and standards.

- neighbourhood forums.

Many anti crime measures are dependent on capital spending which is heavily constrained though estate action is a supplementary allocation which has been used for security measures. Again the problem is not a shortage of good ideas and the following have all proved successful.

It should go without saying that any programme of improvements to improve safety should begin with the characteristics and the problems of each particular estate and should deal with residents priorities. A local authority may fear that residents will want expensive capital solutions when they may want better procedures to deal with racial or sexual harassment.

High rise blocks

The main issues include:

- reducing access points.

- design out recesses which could provide cover for criminals.

- good lighting at all times to corridors, stairwells, entrances and approaches.

- entry phones can be beneficial providing all residents agree to their use.

- introduction of concierge eradicated security problems for tower blocks in Brent.

- creating a garden area around each block with planting and fencing can create defensible space.

- areas under stilts can be filled in and used for communal facilities. In Newcastle, where the city's tower blocks are largely given over to older people, some of these areas have been used to create common rooms and the kind of facilities enjoyed by sheltered housing residents.

Low rise housing

Much of the housing built in the sixties and seventies have been built around ideology rather than knowledge of what people want and how they react to certain spatial patterns. A GLC study published in 1974 contains these words of guidance:

Upon entering the mews proper there is still a change in direction leading...? It is the sense of mystery about what lies around the corner which causes a visitor to question his right to be there - symbolic territory (GLC, 1974).

The glaring error in the GLC statement is in the gender of the visitor. It is not no man's land which is created but no woman's.

The briefest examination of the plans of many 1960s and 70s estates, such as Marquess Road, Mozart, Aylesbury or Angel Town shows how poorly they are linked to their surrounding areas... Once within it, the spatial structure of the estate is often confusing to visitors - another disincentive to using it as a route to anywhere else. The result is that only people who live on the estate are to be found in its public spaces... All this adds up to a situation where the individual housewife, when in public space, is likely to find herself alone. Increasingly, from the 1960s onwards, this has become a potentially dangerous situation. It is made worse because many public buildings, either because the main rooms of these are turned away from public space, or because they are separated from it by areas of landscaping, or both. The consequent lack of informal surveillance of the public space heightens its potential danger. Even where no actual danger exists, women have learned to interpret spaces like these as menacing, and have consequently learned to avoid using them unless strictly necessary. The isolating effects of such a spatial system are obvious (Bentley and Teague, 1989: 4-5).

Footpaths

Footpaths should be set out in consultation with residents and should follow desire lines where possible. Footpaths should take direct routes wherever possible unless they are intended for recreational purposes. The majority of pedestrians are women: women with shopping bags; with young children to control; elderly women; disabled women. Meandering paths are tiring.

• Visibility should be good.

• Avoid heavy planting right up against the footpath creating the fear of hidden attackers. If there has to be planting this should be separated from the path by fencing.

• Consideration should be given to alternative routes for day and night . A footpath which produces no anxieties in daylight may not be so attractive at dusk. An alternative route could allow the pedestrian to walk along a main road at night.

Planting

When considering planting their impact on play spaces, bus stops and footpaths should be carefully considered and species chosen which will not provide dense cover for attackers.

• Maintenance must be regularly undertaken to avoid overgrowing.

• In autumn there should be regular sweeping of leaves to prevent accidents amongst the elderly and those with poor mobility. The same applies to snow clearance.

• Communal open space should be cited near to busy roads and footpaths or should be capable of surveillance by houses. Good facilities are often rendered unusable by women or elderly people because safety factors have not been taken into account.

Lighting

Good lighting can reduce crime and make residents feel safer. Roy Fleming's before and after study of the impact of lighting on crime in Edmonton showed that a before figure of twenty one incidents of assault etc. were reduced to three. Before the lighting was installed 65 per cent of respondents (87 per cent of women) feared for their safety while walking along the dimly lit street or under a railway bridge. After brighter lighting, 62 per cent of all respondents felt safer and 82 per cent attributed this to the lighting (Brimacombe, 1990).

• Lighting is often considered from the motorists view point. This has led to the widespread use of low level sodium lamps whose yellow glow creates shadow and makes colour identification difficult.

• There should be enough lamps so that pools of shadow are not created between lamps.

• Where there are street entry doors or on walls in car parks there should be wall mounted lamps to throw faces into light.

• Rear lanes should also be lit.

• Where there is shrub planting consideration can be given to placing lamps in the bushes.

Women and crime

The British Crime Survey (1982, 1984 and 1988) reveals that those living in multi racial areas of the inner city, non-family areas and poorer council estates experience high levels of victimization. It shows that women and old people (likely to be women) are less likely to be victims of crime than the average man and much less likely than a young man.

Locally based studies reveal that, as important, is how 'crime' and 'victim' are defined. Consider the two tables from Kate Painter's work (1992: 174) the first showing the proportion of men and women experiencing crime and harassment in the borough of Hammersmith and Fulham and on the West Kensington estate while the second examines harassment.

	Borough survey (N = 1,135)		Estate survey (N = 452)		Total	
	Men	Women	Men	Women	Men	Women
Physical assault	6	3	4	7	10	10
Street robbery	6	6	5	5	11	11
Sexual assault	0	1	0	1	0	2
General harassment	19	41	3	18	22	59
Sexual harassment	0	7	0	14	0	21

Women are more likely than men to be victims of general or sexual harassment. The next table details the acts of harassment suffered:

Incident	Men	Women
Stared at	8	17
Followed	5	20
Approached or spoken to by a stranger	5	19
Shouted at or called after	10	20
Touched or held	3	10
Kerb crawled	2	8

It can be seen that most or even all of these acts of harassment are likely to go unreported to the police. Where incidents are reported they are not likely to be investigated and may not be recorded as crimes by the police. Though it is improbable that such incidents will appear in any national picture of crime they cannot be dismissed as minor matters. A woman spoken to suggestively or followed will be afraid that this is simply a precursor to more serious acts. A crucial factor is time of day because an incident which may provoke laughter or challenge in daylight may provoke panic after dark.

Once in the home, women are not free from harassment. Should those who suffer physical beating and rape be discounted there is still a large group of women who are victimized through obscene phonecalls, having underwear stolen from the washing line and being the focus for a peeping tom.

The effect of this victimisation causes women to be careful journey planners during the day and often housebound after dark. Crawford's study in Islington revealed that 43% of women interviewed had been harassed in a public place. Of these 87% who had been victimized once and 97% of those who had suffered a number of times said they were unwilling to use the streets at night (Painter 1992). A study in Birmingham revealed widespread fear among women of using the city centre. Over 60% of women did not go into the city centre after dark.

If you don't go into the city centre after dark why not?

not alone	10%
frightened	58%
not enjoyable	8%
no reason to	8%
no response	17%
too young	4%

If you go into the city centre after dark do you feel safe?

yes	26%
only sometimes	44%
no	27%
no response	3%

(Source: Birmingham City Council, 1990)

Feeling like a victim is a powerful daily social control over women and their movements. The power to wholly eradicate this is not in the hands of planners, nevertheless planners should be alive to the part they can play in creating a safe and welcoming city for both sexes:

It quickly became obvious that women have a different geography of the city to men... their journeys, where they spend their time, why they use the city, etc. Public life is seen as male and the female geography of the city is far from the minds of those who plan and design it (Powell, 1990) [my emphasis].

Sheffield in its draft UDP talks of:

Where possible the design of streets, environmental improvements, pedestrian routes and areas, cycleways and public spaces should:

(a) make them convenient and safe to use for people with disabilities, the elderly, people with young children and young people; and

(b) maximise the personal safety of pedestrians, particularly women and at night (Sheffield City Council, 1991: BE7) .

Similarly Leicester advises that:

Planning permission will not normally be given for proposals which create an environment which is potentially unsafe, particularly for women, children and elderly people (Leicester City Council, 1990: EN 52).

The Birmingham group had many suggestions to make for making their city centre into a 24 hour city and not one which abruptly becomes 'deserted night time streets cruised by taxis and loud crowds of youths' (Birmingham City Council, 1990: 9). Many of their suggestions focused on culture and the arts including music venues, late opening cafes, street theatre. Anyone who has visited the city of Dublin will appreciate how these elements contribute to a vibrant and safe streetscape.

So far this examination of safety needs has concentrated on moving around the immediate neighbourhood and the city centre. Of equal importance is how women make longer journeys. It is well known that fewer women have a driving licence and those that drive have unequal access to a car. The 'family car' these days is often a company car which is restricted to the man while the woman has to resort to walking or public transport. What problems do women face who venture further afield?

Travelling in safety

Subways as a means of pedestrian and cycle access are a product of a time when there was a disproportionate concern for fast, uninterrupted traffic flow rather than safe movement for women, children elderly people and the disabled: in short, pedestrians.

A survey undertaken by Manchester of users of the forty five subways and tunnels revealed that most women only used the subway reluctantly and then only under certain circumstances. Many women and most of the elderly and disabled people who were interviewed in group discussions said that they would never use a subway because of the security issues. Since subways are intended to provide an alternative to crossing traffic it can only be assumed that some people were unable to make their journey by foot and that others used routes including those which took them into heavy traffic.

The case study from the survey illustrates the typical range of problems presented by subways compounded by poor maintenance and long and short term solutions to the problem. While this example is from Manchester, Sheffield City Council in their draft UDP talk of maximising the safety of pedestrians and suggesting that one of the strategies to be implemented is the closure of subways and creating street level crossings where opportunities arise. (Sheffield City Council, 1991: BE7).

Location: Under Chorlton Road, Hulme, Hillfoot walk to Royce Road.
Description: Concrete box tunnel, long sloping entrances, dog-leg bend at Hillfoot walk side.
Problems: No lighting working inside or at entrances. Visibility is poor due to length of tunnel and bend. Regularly flooded. Much rubbish, litter and graffiti. Inaccessible due to slopes and flooding.
Consultation: 8 people interviewed in subway. Flooding, poor lighting, dirt, litter and crime cited as main problems. People said muggings were common. One woman reported being mugged in the subway. Police advice to pedestrians said to be conflicting - not to use road because of traffic, not to use subway because of personal danger. Said to be well used by women taking children to school. Those interviewed strongly in favour of alternative road crossing.
*Recommendations***:**
Closure: Provide on surface pedestrian controlled crossing system at this junction, with complete traffic standstill function and additional crossing

patrol at school times. Subway should be completely blocked to avoid hiding places.

Interim Measures:

Lighting: Upgrade to maximum illumination as recommended in UK national standards for lighting levels (BS 5489). It is recommended that this be applied both within the subways and on all surrounding pedestrian routes. Drainage: Install larger drainage grids. Facilities: Install signposts indicating directions in all tunnels and paths. Maintenance: Weekly inspection should be carried out as part of a regular recorded maintenance schedule (Source: Manchester City Council Community Safety Unit and Greater Manchester Transport Resource Unit, 1991: 16).

Safer public transport

The over dependence of women, elderly people and disabled people on public transport creates a number of problems for these groups. In recent years many of the practices which were seen to benefit more vulnerable groups have been reversed: cheaper fares, conductors on buses, integrated transport systems, improvements to stations. Deregulation of bus services, cuts to British Rail subsidies and a new focus on profitability make journeys by public transport less easy and more expensive (Bashall, 1987). The measures needed are fairly straightforward what is often lacking is the political will and awareness of the issues to bring them about:

• Staff at stations. Tyne and Wear Metro have experienced a number of problems from graffiti and criminal damage to attacks on passengers at stations and on Metro cars. This has been tackled in a number of ways. Firstly, each station has a help point which is primarily for information but is also used by anxious passengers to maintain a voice link with the control centre. Secondly, groups of revenue inspectors move round the network checking tickets but also providing on train surveillance. In addition police dedicated to the Metro system patrol late night trains to increase passenger safety. Many passengers would welcome staffed stations throughout the network but the cost is a deterrent. Extra revenue expenditure would probably cause fare increases causing fewer passengers to travel thus decreasing safety for all.

• Moving bus stops to areas of evening activity creating surveillance at no extra cost.

• Changing bus services to hail and ride schemes. Deregulation has increased flexibility in some town and cities. Hail and ride schemes allow passengers to choose where they feel safe in waiting for the bus. Stockport has changed its less well used routes to hail and ride for the evening and reported an increase in passengers as well as increased passenger satisfaction (Trench, Oc and Tiesdell, 1991).

• Mini buses penetrating residential areas. Many estates were built on ideologies that included the creation of vehicle free zones. The idea was that pedestrian safety would increase, instead many pedestrians now fear the walk, often badly lit and meandering, from the bus stop to home. The long term answer is the return to simple street patterns but one where cars are slowed and made subservient to pedestrians. In the short term public transport can be introduced into residential areas increasing mobility and surveillance.

• Single sex services: Bradford has a 'Homerunner' schemes which started in October 1989 for the use of low income women, black women, disabled women, elderly women, women shift workers, women going to and from evening classes and young women whose previous attack history was such that without the service they would not go out. This is a door to door service operating between 6pm and 11pm Monday to Saturday with a flat fare of 90 pence. The scheme has between 3-400 users per week most of whom use it to travel from home to work and back (Trench, Oc and Tiesdell, 1991).

Cost is a big deterrent in setting up such a service: the Bradford scheme receives a two thirds subsidy on its operating costs which makes it unhealthily dependent on the local authority. However, there is an argument to be made that women only services should be subsidised in the same way and on the same grounds as rural services as these people are transport poor and, without such a service, would not travel at all and suffer loss of quality of life.

The greater problem about women only services is that they may discourage women from using mainstream services which may escalate danger for those who do and bring into question the viability of some routes presently dependent on women as travellers. The cost factor means that these specialist services are unlikely to grow in sufficient numbers to threaten the viability of other services but they do create a lifeline for those women who might otherwise remain at home denied opportunities. The key to this issue, as with so many others, is not that segregated services are better nor that mainstream providers should plan with more sensitivity but that when transport issues are discussed women should be involved in the decision making process. The choice of solution is not as important as who makes the decision.

Access - what access?

Before I was in a wheelchair I used to like going out. It is a very rare event for me these days. It takes so much courage to screw myself up to do battle with an inhospitable environment (DoE, undated).

This is the view of one disabled citizen but this is not a lone voice. Consider the following article appearing in Newcastle's *Evening Chronicle* :

Survey highlights problems for disabled in city

Disabled people face a life of misery on the streets of Newcastle, according to a new survey. It says that for the disabled, many buildings are out of bounds, broken pavements are like assault courses, and, perhaps worst of all, the attitudes of many other shoppers and business people leave a lot to be desired. Sandyford Disability Services's report on its survey into city life for the disabled also says:

- Little is done to help the blind or partially sighted.

- City centre parking could be improved.

- Disabled people have to be jugglers to manoeuvre doors and shopping.

- Shop doors are too heavy for people on crutches and sticks.

- Access problems limit job opportunities for the disabled.

The conclusion of the survey which concentrated mainly on problems in the Sandyford area of Newcastle, is that there is still much more to be done to improve conditions for disabled people in the city. Sandyford Disability Service investigated 17 shops, eight entertainment centres, two churches, schools, blocks of flats and a library. "It does not pretend to be a professional survey, but merely seeks to explore the real problems of access for disabled people by a collection and compilation of facts", says the report. The study found two schools - St. Theresa's and Christ Church primaries in Shieldfield - were virtually inaccessible to wheelchair users and neither have toilets for the disabled.

Of the entertainment venues, the new Warner Brothers complex at Manors and the Ouseburn Watersports Centre are tailor-made for the disabled, says the report. But public houses present many problems, especially with regard to access. Tower blocks in Shieldfield desperately needed alterations to the lift controls and entrance doors were too heavy for both the elderly and the disabled. Of 10 shops surveyed in Shieldfield, only three are accessible to wheelchair users, with only one out of seven shops accessible in Heaton Road. Churches also suffered from poor access and no special toilets. While attitudes of the public were criticised, staff in shops and other buildings were praised. "Access for the disabled in Sandyford is reminiscent of a snakes-and-ladders board, with more snakes than ladders", says the report. If disabled people are lucky enough to be able to enter buildings, they inevitably have no access to toilets, cannot reach any other than the ground floor and are met with an obstacle course in an attempt to move around the building. The report says a register should be compiled to give details of sources of funding available to improve access for disabled (Blackhall, 1989).

The London Borough's Disability Resource Team sum it up:

In Britain today, millions of people are physically prevented from entering buildings, streets, and open spaces as a result of the thoughtless attitudes of developers, planners, architects and other professionals. The ramifications of our inaccessible environment for people with disabilities include discrimination and conflicts in moving around freely, pursuing a social life, obtaining and retaining employment and (consequently) avoiding poverty (LBDART, 1991).

A visitor to Newcastle might wonder how a person in a wheelchair was able to buy books. Only one bookshop, intended mainly for student use, has the bulk of its stock on one floor and slight changes of level within the shop are ramped. All the doors are heavy plate glass and disabled access between the shelves is awkward. Of the others, one has a high step at the entrance and cluttered floor space, the others are on multiple floors offering no customer lift access. While staff may be helpful this does not compensate for the pleasure of browsing. No one doubts the cost of installing a fair sized passenger lift with low level controls nevertheless planners must insist or insist and assist with grant aid.

The issue of accessible shopping facilities raises some interesting questions. Is the poor level of access due to lack of awareness of the needs of disabled people? Is it that disabled people are expected only to shop accompanied by an able bodied person? Is it that those writing the brief and those designing are aware that many disabled people have little money to spend (Barnes, 1991: 98-123) and therefore there is no return on the investment? Design that excludes those in wheelchairs also excludes parents with young children. What is the excuse for this? The Daily Telegraph (1992) ran a campaign to draw attention to the unfriendly environment, suggesting that exposure to poor publicity would create impetus for change:

> Why are the streets full of unwanted children? Every day millions of parents go shopping in the high streets. Their custom may be wanted but their children unfortunately are not. Swing doors that will not budge, impossible staircases, disapproving shop assistants, staff only lavatories, unfriendly restaurants and unwelcoming hotels. The assault course of thoughtlessness is as long as it is depressing. Thankfully, The Daily Telegraph Parent Friendly Campaign, devised in conjunction with Tommy's Campaign, has been launched to help those beleaguered parents fight back. And through the Parent Friendly Awards scheme you can nominate those companies that genuinely try to help and expose those that don't. With the country watching they will have to take action (*Daily Telegraph* in BBC, 1992).

Local authorities as well as newspapers have developed ways of highlighting good practice and creating pressure on others to make improvements.

Sandwell MBC supports a shopmobility drop in centre in Queens Square, West Bromwich from which disabled shoppers may borrow manual or electric operated wheelchairs for the duration of their shopping trip. In addition the council has produced a shopmobility guide for West Bromwich Town Centre. The key to the guide and a sample page are set out on the next two pages. The guide, though excellent in principle, could have been improved by a more thoughtful layout. Both positive and negative features are set out together with only one symbol to draw attention to them. Perhaps separating the positive from the negative and using tick and crosses or snakes and ladders would indicate which facilities presented least difficulty. Parents with babies and small children would benefit from a similar guide showing location of play areas, in-shop creche, unobstructed entrances and lavatories with baby change facilities.

the key to your shoppers guide

Obstruction on entry

Access is particularly difficult or complicated

Flat main entrance/access

Assistance on request

Internal or external steps up

Internal or external steps down

Flat/ramped access everywhere

Special designed toilet for wheelchair users

Possible reach problems

Cafe/restaurant facilities accessible without steps

Narrow aisles

Flat/ramped access to part of the shop/store

Difficulty at the check-out

SHOP	🎞	⚠	M	🧤	🏭	🛗	♿	WC	TWC	⊞	♿	⇥	♿	▤
COLOURVISION Farley Centre *TV & Video Hire*			✱	✱			✱	✱						
LUNN POLY High Street *Travel Agent*			✱	✱			✱	✱						
STELLA VISION High Street *Video Film Hire*			✱	✱			✱		✱					
CAVENDISH High Street *Newsagents*				✱			✱	✱						
ADAMS High Street *Childrens Wear*			✱	✱				✱	✱					
EVANS High Street *Ladies Fashions*			✱	✱			✱		✱					
PEACOCKS High Street *Family Fashion & Household Linen*			✱	✱				✱	✱			✱		
DOROTHY PERKINS High Street *Ladies Fashions*			✱	✱					✱		✱	✱		
THE LEEDS High Street *Building Society*	✱		✱	✱			✱							

There are signs that, in some respects, access for is improving. A walk along many of out towns and city streets will reveal the gulf between those buildings created or adapted since 1985 and those which pre-date the building regulations and yet much remains to be done.

Part of the problem is weak legislation and poorly worded planning powers which leaves the fight for access as a matter of individual or corporate will:

A further problem lies in the encouragement of planners by the existing legal framework of over reliance on colleagues in building control. As everyone knows by the time as development has been submitted for building control scrutiny it is rather too late to contemplate major change. The way forward is for planners to use plan making to set out their stance and to set the tone for development

The planning and design of the City has a very real effect on the quality of life for the disabled and their families. It can place barriers in the way, or it can work to remove barriers. It can allow work, shopping or recreation facilities to exclude the person with a disability, or it can strive to enforce legislation, to educate, and to provide, and thereby to increase the facilities available (Sheffield City Council, 1989).

Sheffield in its draft UDP clearly states on every possible occasion that buildings must be accessible by disabled persons and more specifically states:

BE5 Access to Buildings used by the Public: In all buildings used by the public the following principles will normally apply: New and Refurbished Buildings (a) buildings should include suitable design for access and internal movement for people with disabilities, people with young children and elderly people. (b) other supporting measures such as suitable toilet facilities, childcare and baby changing facilities and seating should be integral part of the design. (c) wherever possible, new development should be sited and designed to make it easily accessible to public transport users. Existing buildings (d) access to existing buildings and their surroundings should be improved as opportunities arise through alterations and extensions to enable all users to move around easily (Sheffield City Council, 1991: BE 5).

Ealing in a now famous appeal successfully enforced their planning policy which stated that access for disabled persons was a priority. Since these aims were set out in Ealing's plan the developer should have been aware of their strategies (Millerick and Bate, 1991):

When planning applications are made for new and existing buildings, the Planning Division will use every opportunity to see that access is incorporated where it previously did not exist. This applies to all buildings to which the public has access including shops, banks, post offices and all other public buildings. Parking spaces and public conveniences for people with disabilities will be included in these requirements.

Transport

Transport is the key to quality of life and participation in life for people with disabilities. Transport is not just about how you choose to get from A to B, it is also about whether you go out at all. It is about being able to use the facilities and opportunities of the City *or* not (Sheffield City Council, 1989).

The Derbyshire Coalition for Disabled People has produced a seven point key to complete social integration, one point of which is 'the encouragement of accessible public transport' (Nuttgens, 1991).

Evidence produced by two studies undertaken in Newcastle upon Tyne indicate to what extent that goal has been realised.

Transport and the visually impaired

The first study (Mitcham, 1992) asks how suitable public transport is for those who are blind or partially sighted. While those with motor impairment can use adapted cars, albeit at cost (Barnes, 1991), the blind together with those who have learning difficulties are dependent on public transport for independent travel. A survey undertaken by Newcastle City Council in 1985 proved that while only 55 per cent of blind and partially sighted people were able to use public transport, those who did use it preferred the bus to the Metro system. Metro is Tyneside's rail based rapid transport system with level access from train car to platform for pushchair and wheelchair as well as waiting space under shelter. By counting the stops it is possible to accurately plot a journey and a warning buzzer alert passengers that doors will close. The bus service in Newcastle can boast of only ten per cent of stops protected by shelters; many stops are just posts which are difficult to locate for those without sight and the practice of missing out stops makes it trying for a blind passenger working out the route. In spite of these obvious difficulties the bus proved more popular in 1985: a further survey undertaken by Mitcham in 1992 demonstrates an equal preference for the bus services many of which have now taken up the recommendations put forward by the Disabled Persons Transport Advisory Committee (DPTAC) which set out voluntary guide-lines in 1988 covering:

- external appearance and route indication
- steps and stairs
- doors and handrails at entrances and exits
- seats
- equipment for information and communication to passengers.

Mitcham's work indicates the widespread take up, by the various bus companies operating in the city, of the recommendations. The survey revealed that the biggest problem for the blind and partially sighted was determining the bus number and many respondents simply flagged down every bus and asked the driver. Once on the bus the disabled passenger had to rely on the driver remembering to call out when their stop is reached.

The Metro presented far more problems to the visually impaired:

• The lack of a tactile strip near the edge of the platform made passengers afraid of falling onto the track. British Rail also fails to provide this inexpensive safety feature. On Metro, the outdoor stations have a groove running along the platform edge but this is not easily felt by a blind person. Underground stations have a black painted line and no tactile band at all.

• The time given for exit and entry is too short for a blind person to locate the door release button and step in or out. The actual time allowed can be as short as ten seconds.

• The train destination is shown on an indicator board but the lack of an announcement station means there is no way of knowing, for a blind person, which train is arriving. Given that there is a tannoy system for passenger information it would be a small step for destinations of trains to be announced.

• The recent introduction of a 15 pence fare for previously free travelling elderly and disabled people means that blind people must locate the ticket machines and follow a complex set of instructions (available on audio tape) in order to buy a ticket.

Criticisms levelled at both bus and Metro systems focused mainly on the lack of information for the blind which could be overcome by:

• a braille timetable at stops and stations or at least a large print version.

• announcements at Metro stations telling passengers the train destination.

• announcements on buses to indicate where the bus has reached.

Transport and the elderly

A study conducted among the elderly (Barber, 1992) revealed far greater enthusiasm for the Metro system because of its level access. The bus service, on the other hand, was criticised by the arthritic as presenting too many difficulties. The lowered steps and the split level steps still proved too high for many elderly people. The Metro while presenting easy access has its own problems the chief of which are the lack of any toilet facilities and the very small lift car giving problems to both wheelchair users and to parents with pushchairs and prams.

For those elderly or disabled persons unable to use the bus or the Metro because of the route, Tyne and Wear Transport Executive operate a 'Care Call' system. To join the scheme the individual must declare why they cannot use other transport. Once registered the passenger becomes eligible for three main benefits:

- Taxi Vouchers: bought in books of ten and having a face value of £1 but costing the purchaser 66 pence each. These are used to pay for taxi rides using the Care Call registered taxis. Generally these are used for hospital visits where an ambulance cannot be provided. This is a way of the state pushing responsibility and cost onto the individual and given that many elderly and / or disabled persons may make frequent hospital visits even with concessionary fares this form of transport imposes a financial burden.

- Care Bus: The passenger waits at the care bus stop and gets on. These buses have wheelchair lifts and deviate from their routes to take passengers to the door of their destination.

- Care Call: This is a door to door mini bus adapted to take wheelchairs. This service needs to be pre booked. Tyne and Wear PTE insist that a passenger needs only to make their booking two days in advance and that 800 people daily use the service for shopping and pleasure trips. This is in marked contrast with statistics for London Dial A Ride service: in 1989/90 where users were only able to book a return journey every 10.4 weeks (Barnes, 1991). Care Call, unlike many other similar systems will allow an elderly or disabled person to travel with a companion though this restriction must hinder family outings.

As in the case of providing safe transport for women, it might be felt that segregated transport leads to main stream service providers ignoring the needs of the elderly and disabled. Evidence from Newcastle suggests that specialist bus services may have stimulated greater awareness and increased the adherence of other providers to DPTAC guide-lines.

Conclusion

In matters of safety and accessibility there is evidence of sensitive thinking and policies being integrated into plans to ensure greater choice for all citizens. There is little room for complacency as all too often planners voice that they have enough to do without picking up on disability or women's issues. Citizens need to lobby their planning authorities to make their voices heard and those educating the planners of the future need to open their eyes to the very real needs who through our thoughtlessness are often forced to stay at home out of sight and out of mind.

References

Barber, W. (1992), "Examining the needs of elderly people for public transport in Newcastle", Option study for the B.A. degree in Town Planning, Department of Town and Country Planning, Newcastle University.

Barnes, C. (1991), *Disabled People in Britain and Discrimination*, Hurst, London.

Bashall, R. (1987), "How women can be free to move", *Town and Country Planning*, October: 274-275.

Bentley, I and Teague, H. (1989), "Gender Bias and Spatial Structure", *Urban Design Quarterly*, October: 3-5.

Birmingham City Council, (1990), *Women in the Centre: Women, Planning and Birmingham City Centre.*

Blackhall, I. (1989), "Life of Misery", *Evening Chronicle*, December 21st, Thomson Newspapers, Newcastle upon Tyne.

Brimacombe, M. (1990), "Shedding light on crime", *Housing*, October: 19-21.

BBC (1992), *Radio Times*, 30th May - 5th June: 45.

Commission for Racial Equality, (1987), *Living in Terror*, CRE, London.

Department of the Environment, (1989), *Tackling Racial Violence and Harassment in Local Authority Housing: A Guide to Good Practice for Local Authorities*, HMSO, London.

Department of the Environment, undated, *On the Level* (video).

Greater London Council, (1974), *Introduction to Housing Layout*, Architectural Press quoted in Boys, J. (1984), "Women and Public Space" in *Making Space: Women and the Man Made Environment*, Matrix Book Group, Pluto Press, London.

Leicester City Council, (1990), Draft Local Plan, October.

Lewis, D. and Maxfield, M. (1980), "Fear in the neighbourhoods: an investigation of the impact of crime", *Journal of Research in Crime and Delinquency*, No 17: 140- 159.

London Borough's Disability Resource Team, (1991)," A Right not a Privilege", *Community Network*, Autumn.

Millerick, M. and Bate, R. (1991), "I Can, Planners Can", *Housing and Planning Review*, June/July.

Planning for Women Group, Manchester City Planning Department, (1987), "Planning a safer Environment for Women", Manchester City Council.

Manchester City Council Community Safety Unit and Greater Manchester Transport Resource Unit, (1991), *Pedestrian Subways and Personal Safety.*

Mitcham, C. (1992), "How accessible is public transport for the blind in Newcastle?", Option study for the BA degree in Town Planning, Department of Town and Country Planning, Newcastle University.

Newcastle City Action Team, (1992), Comments from interviewing team, West End City Challenge household survey.

Nuttgens, P. (1991), "Breaking Down the Barriers", *Search*, Joseph Rowntree Foundation, 11th November: 20.

Painter, K. (1992), "Different Worlds" in Evans, D.; Fyfe, N.R. & Herbert, D.T. (eds), *Crime, Policing and Place: essays in environmental criminology*, Routledge, London.

Powell, H. (1990), quoted in Birmingham City Council, opus cit.

Sheffield City Council (1989), Guide-lines on Disadvantaged Groups and their Needs - Client Sub-Group, November).

Sheffield City Council (1991), Draft Unitary Development plan, February.

Skogan, W. (1987), *Disorder and Community Decline*, Centre for Urban Affairs and Policy Research, Northwestern University, Evanston, Illinois.

Trench, S. & Oc, T. & Tiesdell, S. (1991), Safer Cities for Women - Perceived Risks and Planning Measures, Paper given at the AESOP and ACSP conference, July, Oxford, England.

Chapter 8

Access to utilities: Water, energy and telecommunications

Simon Marvin

Utility firms ... 'inflexible' over repayments

> The heavy-handed inflexible approach of utility companies... was attacked by the National Consumer Council yesterday. Higher charges for poorer consumers, large deposits and unrealistic payment schedules were common complaints against gas, electricity and water companies. Lady Wilcox, chair of the NCC, said experience had shown that with a little patience, understanding and sensible budgeting most consumer debts could be repaid. Pre-payment gas and electricity meters were more expensive than quarterly billing, even ignoring the cost of travel to buy cards or keys for fuel meters. Demands for deposits for connection were commonly based on commercial credit ratings. One disabled man on income support in London was asked for £122.66 to connect a telephone plus a deposit of between £150 and £700 depending on his credit rating. ... Robert Cattle, deputy chief executive of the National Association of Citizens' Advice Bureaux said: "It is the vulnerable and people on low incomes who often bear the brunt of the inflexibility of the utility companies. We are calling on the industry to adopt a more realistic and human attitude to consumers' problems" (The Independent, 1992: 2).

Utility systems provide a crucial link between households and the mainstream of society through a set of water, energy and information flows. The modern city has developed around a series of key infrastructure networks including water, waste, energy and telecommunications. In 1991-92 the average household spent just under £1000 on the package of utility services with total domestic expenditure of around £21,000 million. It would be difficult to imagine how cities would perform in social, economic, or environmental terms without these essential life support systems.

Although research shows that the vast majority of consumers are satisfied with the overall quality of service they receive from their utility (NCC, 1991a) it cannot be assumed that all households have equal levels of access to utility services. More than 2 million homes are not even connected to the telephone network seriously limiting their potential for seeking employment, making complaints about services or calling for help in emergencies. Millions of householders cannot afford to heat their poorly insulated homes to an acceptable level. The new phenomenon of water poverty threatens householders with large families or medical conditions that require larger than average water consumption. There are important variations in domestic levels of connection to, and the quality of service received from utility services. Low levels of access cause thousands of low income households severe social, economic, health and psychological difficulties seriously affecting the quality of their domestic life. These problems are compounded for the elderly, single parent families and the disabled.

Restructuring in the utilities sector

Levels of accessibility to utility systems have not been a major social policy issue but a series of trends are likely to place accessibility on to the social policy agenda. The major cause for concern has been the privatisation and liberalisation of the key utility systems since the early 1980s. Privatisation has radically altered the relationships between the new utility companies and their customers. Since the early 1980s all the major utility networks have been subject to a round of restructuring through a programme of privatisation and liberalisation. This has left cities with a patchwork of different and often competing companies who, together with new entrants, offer a range infrastructure services. The fragmentation of control in the sector has brought about important changes in the way in which infrastructure services are now provided in British cities. There has been a shift away from national performance targets, standards and the universal service obligations of the old nationalised corporations. There are a number of areas of concern.

Privatisation of the public utilities has been accompanied by the introduction of an independent tier of regulators - Ofwat, Ofgas, Offer and Oftel. They are responsible for price and competition regulation and the protection of consumer interests through monitoring of codes of practice and dealing with consumer grievances. The regulators have not been involved in monitoring levels of access to the networks amongst different socio-economic groups. They have developed quality of service indicators, such as the development of an appointments service and setting levels of compensation when specified performance criterion are broken. These issues may be relevant to the concerns raised by affluent consumers but they fail to address the problems faced by low income households. Although the regulators have been involved in the development of disconnections policies and the provision of special services for the elderly and disabled they have positively rejected the approach taken in the US where special tariff and service options have been developed to increase levels of access and service for low income consumers.

The utilities have embraced the concept of the pay-per principle to the consumption of utility services. Customers pay for the service according to their level of use and the costs of providing the service rather than through a flat rate charge for cross-subsidised services. There has been increasing concern that the pay-per principle has been used to justify excessive tariff increases in the domestic sector. The utilities argued that prior to privatisation, residential charges were being underwritten by commercial and business charges to extend the domestic networks and levels of connectivity. The regulators have accepted the thrust of these arguments by allowing the utilities to increase domestic tariffs to a level where they consider that the subsidy has ceased. These price raises have caused major difficulties for millions of low income households and there are now commentators and consumer groups who have argued that high domestic charges are underwriting costs in the business sector where there are increasing levels of competition.

New forms of metering technology are being introduced by the utilities which could provide opportunities for new forms of demand management and extra information on consumption patterns for consumers. For instance pre-payment meters help the utilities to avoid debt, arrears and disconnection and they can also assist consumers in budget planning. However, a key concern is the extent to which consumers in low income and vulnerable groups are self-disconnecting from the supply on cost grounds. Self-disconnection is not monitored and no agency has any data on the frequency and duration of absent supply. Pre-payment technology is already being extended from the electricity into the gas and water sector where there is wide spread concern about the dangers of health and disease complications from self-disconnection.

Finally, most of the new entrants in the gas, electricity and telecoms markets are directing their services at the commercial sector. Residential consumers still have no choice in the selection of alternative gas, electricity or water utilities and only very limited choice in the telecoms sector. Although Mercury do provide a residential service a customer still has to be connected to the BT network and will only make cost savings if they make large numbers of long-distance calls. However, cable companies are offering telephone services to subscribers of cable television entertainment services. The new entrants, Mercury and Sprint in the telecoms sector and US gas companies are orientated at large business users.

Taken together this package of trends in the 1990s point to serious problems for many low income and vulnerable groups in there dealings with the utility services. There is increasing concern from voluntary, consumer and interest groups that many people will suffer serious forms of fuel, water and telephone poverty in the face of changes that are taking place in the utility sector.

Access to utilities: local policy issues

Despite the key role of these systems in sustaining modern urban life there are few direct linkages between local authorities and levels of public access to utility services. However, this was not always the case. In the nineteenth century city it was largely accepted that some form of regulation or municipal enterprise was necessary to prevent wasteful duplication of utility systems, ensure that the essential inputs for industrial production were available and that consumers were protected from excessive charges. Nationalisation of the major utility systems in the late 1940s largely took the issue off the local policy agenda. Public ownership allowed central government to establish broad policy targets for the utilities that ensured that the networks were extended into rural areas and domestic levels of connection increased through cross-subsidisation from the commercial and industrial sectors. In the 1990s why should local policy makers be concerned about levels of access to utility services?

The privatisation and liberalisation of utility services which stimulated a political response from a number of local authorities. For instance, in the run up to water and electricity privatisation, Sheffield City Council mounted an unsuccessful legal challenge to obtain some compensation for their pre-nationalisation municipal utility assets. Since privatisation South Tyneside MBC have publicly raised the difficulties that low income households such as the elderly have had in paying increased domestic utility charges. These campaigns have helped to raise awareness of the local implications of utility privatisation amongst local authorities, voluntary groups and the private sector. This debate even helped to stimulate an article in a local newspaper which published a guide for consumers explaining how they could legally ignore bills and avoid payment for between 5 weeks for BT and by one year for the local water company (The Journal, 21st January 1992).

There is also the potential to translate changes in levels of access to the networks into socio-economic policy indicators. Connection to the networks are so important in sustaining urban life that levels of access to utility systems are used as a surrogate indicator of physical household condition. The incidence of an internal toilet was used as the main indicator to target areas for a range of inner city policies. This indicator has recently been replaced in the census by the incidence of central heating systems based on connection to, and use of energy infrastructure. When central heating is available to over 95 per cent of households perhaps the replacement indicator will be the level of household telecommunication connection eventually signalling the shift from a water, energy, to an information household economy.

Data on levels of access to utility networks is usually only available at a national or regional scale which tends to mask important local variations in levels of access. For instance the Today programme on Radio 4 reported the case of a 23 storey block of flats in Smethwick where 1 in 7 households had been disconnected from the water supply and excrement was being wrapped in packages and then thrown out of windows. There is also evidence that the 2 million households who are not connected to the telephone networks tend to be focused in particular places. It was reported that the level of household connection to the telephone network dropped to 46 per cent on a Northumbrian coalfield council estate (RDC 1989). Variations in the location of fuel poverty have long been recognised because of the role of poorly constructed, designed and insulated house types which tend to be concentrated in particular estates. These problems may be even further compounded by DSS cold weather payments which are made on the basis of temperature readings at regional monitoring centres which are linked to a large number of postcode districts. Serious anomalies occur when an estate is split by postcode districts which are linked to different monitoring stations triggering cold weather payments for one set of households but excluding others even though the local temperature is low for all homes.

These wide micro-spatial variations in levels of access to utility systems raise a number of key issues and problems for local authorities. If relatively large numbers of households in a particular area are disconnected from the water supply there are potentially serious health and environmental implications for the area. Similarly high levels of fuel poverty are likely to be linked to medical and health problems for residents. Low levels of telephone ownership limit the ability of the most vulnerable groups to maintain social contacts, complain about local services or enquire about eligibility to welfare benefits. An even more disturbing problem is the extent to which households suffer from multiple forms of low accessibility to utility networks. Although no research has examined this issue it is quite likely that the same low income families have difficulties heating their homes and paying for metered water while also doing without a telephone.

Utility networks played an important role in the disturbances in the West End of Newcastle and the Meadow Well estate in North Tyneside at the end of 1991. It was reported on the Today Programme (Radio 4, March 1992) that in the early phase of the disturbance on the Meadow Well rioters set fire to a local electricity sub-station plunging the area into darkness as the street lights were extinguished. Later the local telephone service was deliberately disabled preventing all incoming and outgoing telephone calls. Disconnection from both these sets of services was used a means of isolating the Meadow Well by seriously disrupting the ability of local residents to call and the emergency services to respond to the disturbances. Ironically there is evidence that the areas were rioting took place have some of the lowest levels of connection to the telephone network and lowest levels of household energy consumption in Tyneside.

In most cities there is now a patch work of different companies responsible for utility services each having their own tariff and customer care policies. For instance 33 per cent of households have their water and sewerage service provided by different companies. There are already local variations in water and sewerage charges and in the near future this could be extended to domestic gas and electricity pricing. Each of the regional companies have adopted different customer codes of practice and even national organisations such as British Gas and British Telecom regional managers have considerable autonomy in their policies for domestic consumers. It can no longer be assumed that there are nationally agreed levels of service standards and tariff arrangements in one particular city. Instead it is quite likely that different companies will have various policies, tariff levels and methods of payment perhaps causing consumers some confusion.

Access to utilities: towards a conceptual model

A key feature of the increasing concern about the socio-economic implications of restructuring in the utility sector for particular social groups has been the recognition of the common features and characteristics of utility supply issues. There are a number of properties of utility services that distinguish them from normal market commodities (Ernst 1991, National Consumer Council 1989). These features are:

- necessities for life
- non-substitutability
- inelasticity of demand
- natural monopolies
- regulation.

At the household level water and energy services are amongst the core necessities for live. The development of water, sewerage and energy services were closely related to improvements in health and overall quality of life. These services are largely non-substitutable as there are no real alternatives to connection to the mains water and sewerage networks in urban areas. Although there are usually two energy sources, gas and electricity, the high equipment conversion costs effectively limit the ability of households to substitute between the systems and alternatives to the BT telephone service are only developing slowly.

All households have to use a certain amount of energy or water regardless of household income or the cost of utility services. Consequently demand for utility services does not rise or fall in proportion to household income and low income households spend proportionately over three times as much on fuel as high income households. This problem is further compounded for those households who for health, social and medical reasons actually need to use more water and energy than the average household.

Although there are increased levels of competition in commercial and industrial markets in the domestic sector utility services are all effectively natural monopolies. There are no alternatives to the local water and sewerage company but with new metering technology it should be possible to use energy infrastructure networks as common carriers for different supply companies. There is already some degree of competition in the domestic telephone market through new entrants such as Mercury and the cable companies. However, it is not clear if domestic customers even want alternative suppliers or whether they will have the necessary data to make informed choices about the alternative services on offer. For the vast majority of households, particularly those on low incomes, utility services will be based on monopoly supply. The key issue is how the customer interest should be regulated given the monopolistic features of utility services and their importance in sustaining modern life. The health, safety, environmental and social implications of utility services cannot be treated as mere commodities which are traded in free markets and they require some form of policy regulation to protect customer interests.

There is increasing recognition of the need to examine the issue of access to utility services as a package of related issues. For instance the Public Utilities Access Forum (PUAF 1991) was established in 1989 to 'collaborate in drawing the particular needs of consumers with low incomes to the attention of the water, electricity, gas and telecommunication industries, their Regulators, and other relevant bodies'. Although the initial focus was on gas and electricity systems it has more recently taken an interest in water and telecommunications. The Forum has played a key role in co-ordinating the concerns raised by voluntary and community groups, developing clear policy objectives and debating issues with the regulators.

Any attempt to develop measures of levels of access to utility services requires a clear conceptual model of the problem (see Lucy 1981). Public policy has tended to use crude indicators of levels of access such as connection and disconnection rates rather than considering other more subtle problems such as self disconnection from pre-payment meters. However, the interest in issues which cut across all the utility services has created an opportunity for developing a broader conceptual model of levels of access.

The table below provides a framework against which policy makers can start to think through different forms of access to utility systems. The framework is developed in the following way. Firstly, before each of the systems can be used consumers need a live connection to the network. Consequently one measure of access is the levels of connection to the network which can be measured in a number of different ways. Secondly, if a consumer is connected to the network various use of service indicators can be examined to provide measures of the quality of service to particular socio-economic groups. Finally, the last set of measures provide some indicators by which the implications of non-connectivity or low levels of service use can be assessed. Although a household may be connected to a particular network a combination of low income and poorly insulated home means that it does not obtain a comparable level of comfort for a similar energy input into an insulated home. This model identifies a number of indicators that are common to all infrastructure systems and allow policy makers to measure and monitor levels of access and quality of service for households.

Accessibility to utility networks: examples of indicators

CONNECTION

- Connections to service   percentage households connected
- Network investment   £ per 1000 population or households
- Special facilities   fibre optic cable per household

USE OF SERVICE

- Use by amount	number litres of water consumed per day
- Use by rate	electricity consumed pa by household
- Method of Payment	prepayment, credit, standing charges, repayment of arrears, budget tariffs, deposits
- Quality of Service	pollution, unavailability, interruptions
- Non-use of service	fear of debt, concern about costs

IMPACTS

- Medical	hypothermia, disease, illness and death
- Social	isolation, age, size of family, theft, low level of consumption & service, anxiety & worry
- Economic	debt, arrears, disconnection, low tariff schemes
- Environmental	housing conditions, emissions

Service levels according to need are based on the concept that those with unequal needs should be treated unequally. Low income groups such as the elderly, disabled and single parent families need more water and energy than the average household. They are likely to be at home all day, need higher than average temperatures and use more water for health and washing. A range of service indicators could be developed to provide a measure of need. However, in the utility sector these indicators are generally not used to allocate services. There is one major exception. The regulators recognise that the elderly and disabled have problems reading awkwardly sited meters and are more susceptible to attempts by criminals to impersonate utility workers. Consequently a number of schemes have been adopted to provide special services to the elderly and disabled if they are requested. For instance under the term of BT's licence the company has to pay special attention to the needs of elderly and disabled consumers; in 1990 British Gas prepared a code of practice for the elderly and disabled; in 1991 Ofwat sent model guidelines for elderly and disabled customers to each of the water companies; and, Offer has been approving the codes of practice which the electricity companies are obliged by law to produce. The regulatory frameworks have recognised that the unequal needs of the disabled and elderly require a degree of unequal treatment in the operation of utility company customer policies. A range of special services are offered by utilities to those customers who identify themselves as being elderly or disabled. However, these services have not been developed to meet the particular needs of ethnic minorities and, with the exception of a recent change in BT's tariff structure, there are no tariff reductions for vulnerable or low income customers.

There are three particular social issues, which have important equal opportunities implications, that concern many voluntary, consumer groups,

Customer Service Committees and professional bodies. These are the development of water poverty, the continuation of fuel poverty and low levels of connection to the telephone network. There is increasing concern that as the scale of personal debt among low incomes households rises, the level of social security benefits fall in real terms and that the prices for services rise in the future there could be a significant decrease in levels of access to utility services. If these charges are linked to a shift to prepayment metering as a charging system then self-disconnection from supplies and the consequent implications could become a major social issue in the 1990s.

Floods of water poverty

In the 1990s the affordability of water and waste services is emerging as an important social policy issue. The reasons for the development of these concerns relate to the three key features of water supply that do not apply to other utility systems (NACAB 1991, NCC 1991b).

• Water supply is more vital than any other infrastructure system.

• Water is the most complete natural monopoly and supply cannot be substituted.

• Lack of supply has personal and wider public health implications.

By 1979, 95.7 per cent of the population were served with sewers, the highest percentage amongst the developed countries of Western Europe and North America. Despite these high connectivity figures substantial numbers of households are not connected to the water or sewerage networks. In 1981 1.2 per cent of the population, 691,000 people, were not connected to the water mains. These figures hide wide levels of spatial variation. In the South West 6.4 per cent of the population were not connected but in the Thames region the figure was only 0.04 per cent. An even higher percentage of the UK population are not connected to main sewers. At 4.7 per cent some 2.6 million people have to find alternative methods of waste disposal. As would be expected the more rural authorities have the highest levels of non-connectivity over 8 per cent in Northern Island, South West, Anglian and Welsh regions (Edwards and Cox, 1982:42). The population not served by mains water and sewerage networks tend to be located in the more isolated rural areas which are expensive to serve through the mains network. It is likely that this residual percentage of homes will not be connected to mains water and drainage as the costs are to high. However, a report by the RDC (1990) found that the water companies probably underestimate the population not serviced by the mains network. Also a significant percentage of the households not connected would like to link to the system to take benefits of a more reliable, efficient and cleaner service. But many potential consumers were not able to afford the costs of connection. Since water privatisation the companies levy an infrastructure charge for the cost of new investment in water treatment and sewage works in addition to charges for connection to the water and waste systems.

There are a number of water quality service indicators as Ofwat (1991a) collects data on various measures including:

- availability of water resources
- percentage of population subject to water restrictions
- pressure of mains water
- interruptions to water supply
- flooding from sewers
- response to billing queries and written complaints

This data indicates that there are important spatially-based variations in levels of service quality across the 39 water companies. How this affect individual consumers will depend on their particular circumstances but for those dependent on kidney dialysis complications with water and electricity supply could be life threatening. Additional performance indicators will be added to the above list over the next two years including drinking water quality, disposal of sewage sludge and levels of water leakage.

There are two new trends in the water industry, increased water charges and water metering, which are giving rise to serious social policy concerns. Water charges have started to increase quite significantly to pay for the estimated £26 billion of investment planned over the next decade to meet European Commission water and waste quality standards. Between 1989-91 the average unmeasured household water bill increased by over 15 per cent and in some water companies the increased was as high as 34 per cent (Ofwat, 1991a). Substantial price rises are envisaged over the next 10 years varying between companies from 22 per cent above inflation to an astonishing 122 per cent. In some companies the increase could be as high as 22 per cent above inflation in one year. There are already significant variations in the charges made by each of the 39 water and sewerage companies.

An indicator of the problems that households are having with water charges are the number of customers disconnected. When people are in debt water companies are required to obtain a court judgement and, if the customer fails to abide by the terms, disconnection follows. This clause was inserted at a late stage in the Water Bill to try to protect customer interests. The number of county court summonses has reached alarming proportions. In 1990-91 there were a total of 900,000 county court summonses and in half these cases court judgments were issued. Compared to the other utility services the threat of water disconnection usually results in payment of the bill, and in the case of a disconnection the supply is soon reconnected. However, in 1991-92 there were over 21,000 disconnections for non-payment of charges representing one disconnection for every 1,000 households billed. This was a 177 per cent increase on the previous year when 7,673 households were disconnected. Levels of disconnection vary dramatically across the water companies with a high of 75 disconnections per 10,000 households billed in South Staffordshire to a low of only 0.21 in Thames (Ofwat News Release, June 1992). Disconnection raises serious health problems for individual households and the wider community.

> If a household has no electricity supply the effects on the household may be catastrophic but only a nominal risk will be placed on the community. In the case of water, however, the risks of any household being without water, or using an inadequate amount of water can have a very real impact, particularly with regard to the transmission of diseases relating to poor hygiene such as gastro-enteritis. Obviously, this social risk is multiplied if any significant numbers of households in a particular area are without water supply or do not use adequate amounts. It is, therefore, essential that a charging structure for water and social policy concerns are not divorced (NACAB, 1991:10).

There is evidence of heavy handed and aggressive approaches being adopted by some water companies. For instance there is evidence of rapid summons issuing often without reminders or final notices being sent causing distress to customers. The £30 cost of the summons and a £37 disconnection charge is added to the debt. These problems are further compounded as the CAB reports unsympathetic attitudes in a number of companies where they have refused to negotiate with the Bureaux and refused to accept offers of payment arrangements. In some cases contact could not be established with a representative from the company. These factors can all lead to a disconnection being made.

> A CAB in East Anglia reports the case of a man on invalidity benefit who was disconnected for non-payment of water charges and, as a consequence, dug holes in the garden for 18 months because he was unable to use the toilet until the local authority finally paid the bill (NACAB 1991:9).

There is increasing evidence that those people on low incomes are finding it much harder to pay as their water charges rise. This is further compounded by insufficient benefit levels which cannot meet peoples needs. Unfortunately data on water arrears is not collected by Ofwat and is not made publicly available by the water companies. If water charges data was collected as a separate item in the Family Expenditure Survey, rather than being included in overall housing expenditure, it would be possible to examine the increasing proportion of low income families expenditure on water charges. Those households who need to use above average amounts of water are also likely to be those who will have greatest difficulty paying for increased water charges. It is unlikely that these needs will be met through the policies currently adopted by the regulator. Ofwat argue that 'it would be unfair to other water customers if general tariff policy were to reflect social objectives. These should be part of health and social service policy. Any costs from providing support to customers with particular need should be met by the appropriate agency, and not by water customers generally' (Ofwat, 1990: 10). However, there is a duty imposed on Ofwat under section 7 (4) of the Water Act 1989 to 'take into account, in particular, the interest of those who are disabled or of pensionable age'. A working group has prepared guidelines on the development of services for the disabled and elderly on the basis that 'no customer should receive a poorer quality of service, by comparison with other consumers, because of their age or disability'. It is recommended that their advice should be incorporated into codes of practice drawn up by each of the 39 companies. However, they are not available in minority languages and do not include tariff reductions. Where the method of charging is related to consumption disabled people can get into serious difficulties. These issues need to be addressed in the formulation of fare and equitable charging strategy.

The problems faced by low income households are likely to intensify. After the 1st April 2000, water and sewerage companies will not be allowed to base charges on the rateable value of properties. In its place a new method of charges will be developed and the metering principle has emerged as the most favoured option within the industry. Water meters are already compulsory fitted into new domestic properties and it is likely that their use will be extended as they are retrofitted into existing properties over the next decade. The concern is that the application of metering and the pay-per principle together with higher water charges will cause low income families and those consumers who have to use above average levels of water severe financial difficulties. Some voluntary groups are already starting to talk about the concept of 'water poverty'. The problem is even further compounded as the industry have taken the view that social issues are the concern of government policy and not the water companies or the regulator

Watercare: services for the disabled and elderly

Register of Customers with Special Needs
Companies should raw up registers of customers vulnerable to supply interruptions, fraudulent callers, disconnection and requiring assistance with billing. Information on kidney dialysis users is available from the health authorities but other information should be volunteered. Registered do not necessarily have to be disabled or retired and they can select which services they need.

Customer Awareness Special Services
Leaflets should be made available to notify customers of special services also available in braille and on audio tape.

ID Scheme
Agreeing a password scheme to be used by company workers.

Billing
Can be made available in braille and tape.

Nominee Scheme
A person can be nominated to help deal with payments and negotiate with the company. They are not responsible for the bill and the company will allow more time to resolve the problem.

Access to Company Buildings, Recreation and Leisure Facilities
Should be fitted with wheel chair access, tactile signs for the blind, facilities
for the deaf and disabled

Meter Siting
All metered customers should be able to check their water meter
consumption at reasonable intervals via meter siting, outreach monitors and
meter reading services.

Provision of Advice on Special equipment
Special equipment, adaptions and aids are available for the elderly and
disabled to use in their kitchens and bathrooms. The companies do not have
to provide this help themselves but should advise customers on the specialist
sources of information.
(Ofwat, 1991b)

Ofwat's review of water charging policy has come down in favour of
water metering. Although there are clearly inequities with the present
system of charging there is evidence that metering is causing major
problems. On the Sheffield Manors estate a recent development of 4000
homes all fitted with water meters a campaign has developed against
metering. There have been reports of substantially increased bills, cuts in
water usage and serious concerns expressed about the potential health
implications.

Local GP Dr Richard Watton is worried about the health of his
patients. 'It would be scaremongering to say there would be an
increase in cholera or typhoid or serious illness, but certainly you can
expect an increase in minor forms of gastroenteritis. ... poor people
on the Manors have to think about whether they bath their children at
night, and I don't think this is fair'. The Institution of Environmental
Health Officers has argued that metering could adversely affect low-
income households. They 'suggest that people who over-economise
could find their homes infested with bed-bugs, fleas or cockroaches;
they could be more susceptible to head lice; and their could be a
greater risk of food poisoning. The risks of diseases such as hepatitis
and typhoid would also be greater adds the institution' (Dobson,
1991:12. & 13).

Disabled people are often in extreme poverty and face serious health
problems. High level of water usage are not necessarily linked to affluence.
Many medical conditions require a high level of water usage through hot
baths in the case of conditions such as arthritis while other, such as
incontinence, also require a large amount of laundry. The OPCS estimate
that there are up to 1 million disabled people who have disabilities affecting
their continence. For example, 550,000 people claimed the laundry
allocation in 1987 under the old Supplementary Benefit System.

> All consumers are dependent on water supplies for individual and public health and for some with disabilities, for example those undergoing renal dialysis at home, their dependence could be greater (NACAB, 1991:1).

A recent report published by Ofwat and the DoE of 6,429 households examined the social impact of water metering . Although the survey found that 91 per cent of households experienced no difficulties as a result of water metering, the sample of households was not typical of the British household structure. For instance in the survey only 6 per cent of households were in receipt of income support a third of the national figure. However, the survey did find that 2.2 per cent of households required additional water for a medical condition such as respiratory illness, arthritis, rheumatism, bowel, stomach and urinary disorders. A third of these households used less water than was actually needed, particularly for bathing. Overall 8.3 per cent of households experienced difficulty as a result of metering. In depth interviews found that:

- the majority of this group worried about their water bills and using too much water.

- this worry contributed to family tension.

- some households had reduced the number of baths and showers by 50%.

- that a high proportion of households who experienced most financial difficulty had 5 or more members.

The companies argue that there is relatively little they can do as their license conditions prevent them from discriminating for, or against a particular groups of customers. They argue that the government should revise the benefits system to take account of the bill paid by customers. But there are no plans from the DSS to help low income families with their laundry bills. Other forms of metering also give cause for concern. It is possible to develop time based meters that provide a service for a fixed time. Although it would be possible to have an emergency credit button it still leaves the problem of self-disconnection.

Fuel poverty

It has been estimated that a total of 2,400 households in the country are not connected to the mains electricity network. Research commissioned by the The Rural Development Commission (RDC, 1990) suggests that these are almost exclusively located in rural areas confined to scattered and isolated premises which are difficult to connect to the mains network. The rate of non-connection to mains electricity is around 0.01 per cent. Only in the South West with 1000 households not connected does the level of non-connection exceeds 0.03 per cent of connections. The gas industry has a much lower penetration rate than the electricity sector with just over 17 million households connected out of a total of some 21 households. The high costs of extending the gas network in rural areas is responsible for this lower penetration rate.

These connection rates have important implications for the levels of service that can be obtained from the networks. Low income households are less likely to have a gas supply. In 1986 only 67 per cent of the 30 per cent of households with the lowest incomes had a gas supply compared with 77 per cent for the other households. Consumers not connected to the gas network have to rely on electric heating, bottled gas, paraffin or other forms of expensive heating. The cost of a unit of warmth from an electric bar fire at peak rates is three times higher than that from gas heating. Although off-peak electric storage heaters can compete with gas high levels of insulation are needed. Consequently, the gas networks needs to be extended to poor households. In urban areas new customers pay a relatively small connection charge subject to the boards expenditure not exceeding £480. If the costs exceed this limit the full cost of the connection is passed on to the customer. However, in rural areas where most of the non-connected households are located costs can be very much higher and even exceed £10,000. Low income households are likely to have difficulties paying the connection charges or persuading a landlord to fit a supply.

The key social policy issue associated with the energy sector is the problem of fuel poverty. Fuel poverty has been recognised as a major social policy issue since the late 1970 (Wicks, 1978). The oil crisis of the early 1970s resulted in major fuel price rises creating serious difficulties for low income households living in poorly insulated homes. Boardman (1991a) defines fuel poverty as the inability to afford adequate warmth because of the energy inefficiency of the home. Low income households live in homes that lack adequate insulation, have inefficient heating systems and use the most expensive fuels. Households on higher incomes cannot afford to invest in extra insulation, purchase efficient heating systems and lower the costs of heating their homes. Low income households simply lack the resources to undertake energy efficiency improvements to their homes.

The 30 per cent of households with the lowest incomes spend 10 per cent of there income on fuel compared with around 4 per cent by the other 70 per cent of households. But even by spending 10 per cent of there income they cannot afford to heat their homes properly and it is accepted that these households, totalling 7 million are in fuel poverty. Boardman (1991a) argues that the figure of 7 million could underestimate the number of homes in fuel poverty but there are probably now 1.5 million more households in fuel poverty than 1980. The elderly, unemployed, single parent families and the disabled are disproportionately likely to be poor and in fuel poverty. These groups are also likely to spend more time in the home and there fuel needs are greater than people at work.

The DSS no longer recognises that households have different levels of energy efficiency. The DSS operate the Cold Weather Payments scheme. During severe weather an eligible claimant can obtain an extra payment of £6 per week. At most 2.6 million households are eligible and then for only one or perhaps two weeks worth of payments. As mentioned above there are serious anomalies in the operation of the scheme when a housing estate is split between two different weather stations. There was a scheme to offer rebates on standing order charges to low energy users. But this was abandoned when it was found that the main beneficiaries where second home owners (Boardman, 1991b).

A key indicator of fuel poverty is the number of households experiencing difficulty paying for gas and electricity supplies (see Boardman, 1991b). Traditionally the main indicator has been the number of disconnections from supply. In the gas of case there was a large increase in disconnections in the run up to privatisation and immediately afterwards. However, overall levels of disconnection are now at there lowest levels for a decade reducing from 140,000 in 1980 to 77,000 in 1990 in the electricity sector. But this reduction in disconnection levels does not mean that less households are having difficulties paying their bills. Under pressure from the regulators and consumer groups efforts are now made in the industry to keep fuel debtors connected to the supply. This is being achieved through the installation of pre-payment meters and the operation of fuel direct.

Pre-payment metering allow consumers to pay for current energy consumption while collecting an outstanding debt. The electricity sector has replaced coin operated meters with more modern token or card operated systems. The gas industry is about to start replacing coin meters with a card operated system. Since 1981 2.5 million households have changed to a prepayment meter to pay for electricity. However, there are number of problems associated with these systems. When customers who are connected to the supply networks through prepayment meters are in financial difficulties they are obliged to 'self-disconnect' themselves till next in pocket or use the system very frugally. The lack of supply is concealed from the public and the regulator, the frequency and duration do not appear in any records and this denies any opportunity for public policy action. In addition it has been found that some customers, particularly the elderly, single parent families and the disabled have difficulties obtaining tokens or cards. They may have to undertake additional, expensive and inconvenient trips to obtain tokens from dispensers sited in electricity or gas board show rooms. Prepayment metering technology provides utilities with a mechanism for ensuring debt repayment and removes the need for disconnections for non payment of bills. However, prepayment technology does not address the underlying problems of need and poverty. It is clear that significant numbers of people remain disconnected for lengthy periods and some almost indefinitely. However, such systems do have some benefit to the consumer as they provide a supply when it might otherwise be denied by the utility. The other mechanism for paying off debt is fuel direct where the debt is paid off by direct payment to the utility out of DSS benefits. The utilities, DSS and consumer agencies have agreed that the maximum repayment rate should be £2 per week as a compromise between the customers ability to pay and utilities need to recover debt.

Fuel poverty has a number of social policy implications (Boardman, 1991b, King 1992):

- the excess winter death rate has ranged from 29,000 in 1986-87 to 55,000 1985-86.

- during the two-week cold spell in February 1991 there 4,000 deaths above the normal winter excess.

- there are an extra 8,000 deaths for every $^{\circ}C$ that winter is colder than average.

- studies have linked infant deaths in winter with low levels of income and expensive heating systems.

- excess winter deaths double for every 9 years of advancing age over 40.

- almost 2 million homes in England have winter temperatures below the World Health Organisation minimum of $18^{\circ}C$. It is suggested that temperatures should be $2\text{-}3^{\circ}C$ warmer for the elderly disabled and very young.

- low temperatures are a major factor in causing damp and condensation.

The problem of obtaining adequate heat cause millions of households, particularly the elderly, disabled and single parent families severe economic, social and health difficulties.

Telephone: low levels of connectivity

Connection to the telephone system is not necessarily as essential as having a water, electricity or even gas supply. But as we shift from an energy to a more information based society the absence of the most basic of telecommunications tools, the telephone, is a serious problem for many households.

> More and more, the telephone is taken for granted - for example, as the standard way of following up advertisements, obtaining information, expressing views (maybe in response to broadcasts) and keeping in touch (Milne, 1990: 365).

The telecoms system has one of the lowest levels of connectivity of all utilities and the UK now has a lower telephone penetration rate than the US, Canada, Australia, Scandinavia, and France. The current penetration level of telephones is between 85 per cent to 87 per cent (Regional Trends, 1991 & Family Expenditure Survey, 1991) means that there are approximately 3 million households without a telephone. But this figure masks some lower penetration rates in particular social groups. Amongst low income groups, the elderly, single parent families and furnished private tenants penetration rates are significantly below the average. The evidence from ACR (1991) and the NCC (1991c) shows that:

- only 60% of households with an income of less than £60 per week have a telephone.

- less than 62% of single parent families have a telephone.

- less than 72% of single pensioners dependent on State benefits have a telephone.

- 27% of households headed by 16-24 year olds did not have telephones.

- 25% of households in social class DE did not have a telephone.

- nearly 1 in 3, 32%, of those renting accommodation did not have telephone.

There is considerable variation in the spatial distribution of telephones. In general the South has more telephones that the North, Wales and Northern Ireland. However, this coarse grained data masks wider disparities that only become apparent at the micro-spatial scale. A 1986 study of socio-economic conditions in Newcastle council wards found penetration rates that ranged from 55 per cent of households to nearly complete penetration in some of the richer wards. A 1992 survey found that connection rates dropped to 26 per cent on Cruddas Park a Newcastle housing estate of some 3,000 households. The limited data that is publicly available indicates that there is considerable variation in penetration rates amongst different socio-economic groups and spatial areas.

Very little is known about the implications of non-connection on households although anecdotal evidence does indicate that it does place them in some difficulties with regard to communication, job applications, isolation and problems with calling the emergency services.

Bill, in his forties, lost his job six months ago. With three children at school, he and his wife decided the phone would have to go. Now, when he rings up about jobs from a call-box the day after the local paper comes out, he finds they've already gone to early birds who rang from home.

June, a single parent, lives alone with her year-old son in a flat on the sixth floor. Since leaving home she hasn't been on the phone. She can't afford the deposit though she sometimes feels very isolated.

Elsie was 92 when she went to bed early with all her clothes on one freezing night. The phonebox outside had been vandalised, so she couldn't call her son to fix the heating.

These stories are fictional, but true stories very like them happen every day in Britain. About 85 per cent of households are now on the phone. That leaves over 3 million households who are not. Among certain social groups matters are much worse - 30 per cent of elderly people living alone are not on the phone (Milne, 1989: 20).

We do not know whether pay phone provision is higher in those areas of low telephone penetration. Low levels of telephone penetration may even result in increased economic costs for the rest of society because households have difficulty in calling the emergency services. It is clear that the apparent shift to more information intensive society will simply pass by many households who are not even connected to one of the most basic of telecommunications tools. The lack of a link into the telephone networks means that these households will also not be able to connect to the new information services.

However, Tinker's (1989a) study showed that telephones provide a crucial service for the elderly and disabled and that while many local authorities and housing providers have focused on the need for alarms the telephone has not assumed as much importance. All the interviewed organisations concerned with the needs of elderly and disabled considered that a telephone was essential. The 100 elderly and disabled people interviewed mainly needed a telephone for emergency purposes although they were also important for maintaining links with families. Most respondents considered a telephone to be of more importance than links with neighbours. It was felt that the telephone is likely to become more important with greater demand from the next generation of elderly and disabled and the spread of home alarm systems which operate through the telephone. Increased accessibility is likely to closely related to the affordability of connection charges.

The barrier to telephone connectivity is composed of a connection charge, possibly a deposit and then the quarterly standing charge and possible telephone rental. The connection charges to the telephone network can very across the country at the discretion of local management between £36 and £180. There is evidence that the unemployed have to pay a very large percentage of the charge up-front before connection to the system and that these vary across the country depending on the discretion of local managers (Milne, 1989). For other consumers the costs involved charged after connection together with the first quarterly line rental. Consequently the costs involved in even connecting to the system could be very substantial causing severe difficulties for those on low incomes. However, BT may also demand long or short term deposits from customers in addition to the connection charge. The deposit can again vary at the discretion of local offices between £75 - £150. Long term deposits can be requested from bad-debtors, but this may refer to an address and not just an individual customer, the unemployed and those with no previous history of telephone connection. Those in rented accommodation are most at risk of being required to pay a long term deposit.

Cost is a key factor in explaining non-connection to the telephone system. The ACR survey (1991) found that 63 per cent of the 242 respondents not connected to the telephone network said the cost of connection was the most important factor where as only 24 per cent stated that they did not need a telephone. There results indicated that 2 out of every 3 non subscribers were put off by the cost. The cost factor was most significant amongst women, those aged 16 - 24 and 35 - 44, social class DE, single parent families and the unemployed. Over 66 per cent of these non subscribers would like a telephone but the main concern was the size of the connection charge and the deposit required. Oftel has now required BT to reduce its connection charge to a maximum of £99 which can be paid over a year. This may still be too large for many low income consumers and there remains concern about the level of deposits required by BT.

In comparison to the US where regulatory commissions collect data on telephone subscribers rates by ethnic group, there is no data on connection and ethnicity in the UK. Local authorities are able to give help to disabled and elderly people for telephone installation, adaption and running costs under the Chronically Sick and Disabled Persons Act 1970. However, the criteria adopted are often quite stringent. Claimants are required to be totally housebound and have no regular support or contact from relatives or neighbours. There may also be medical and financial criteria to be settled. However, one local authority made support available to all people over a certain age as they were deemed to be disabled.

Relatively little is known about the levels of telephone usage amongst different social groups. However, the limited research available does indicate that the main issues involved in use are the costs of tariffs, ease of equipment use and methods of payment. The ACR (1991) survey found that 22 per cent of current consumers were definitely concerned about the cost of telephone services. Concern about the costs was higher for the following groups:

- single parent families.
- those with very young children.
- those in large households with children.
- the unemployed.

> Running through all the interviews was the theme of costs and not being able to afford more than a minimum number of calls. An older male respondent remarked: "For emergency use purposes only, I don't use the telephone very much because I can't pay the bill." And a woman, also in her mid-seventies, with some eye trouble, said: "We can't afford social use since we are pensioners." An 88 year old man who was housebound said the same: "Emergencies only to keep the cost down" (Tinker, 1989b: 39).

The main cause for concern was the cost of rental of line and equipment. Tinker's survey of the elderly and disabled found that telephone usage was low with 84 per cent making only local calls. Very few people were interested in special telephone equipment or innovations despite their needs not being met by conventional telephones. Part of the problem was general lack of information of what was available, they had not seen publicity material and the information which was available was not always very user-friendly. But the man constraint was fear of costs of the telephone equipment and services. But paradoxically they had very little idea of what they actually paid for telephone services. However 80 per cent respondents wanted some form of concession.

There are a range of special telephone services available for the disabled and elderly. In 1986 DIEL was established to provide an independent voice for disabled and elderly customers of telecommunication services and apparatus and advises Oftel on services and equipment policy. **Although BT** makes no special tariff concessions for elderly and disabled customers a range of services are available (see DIEL 1991):

• A free directory enquiry service for customers who are blind, partially sighted, disabled or suffer a medical condition that prevents them using a phone directory can register for free directory enquiry calls.

• Keeping Your Line Open elderly and disabled customers can nominate a person who BT can contact to resolve problems of non-payment if the customer has had to enter hospital.

• A Priority Fault Repair Service available to those who live alone, are housebound, suffer long term sickness and disability, or require access to dialysis machine or artificial ventilator.

• A free guide to special equipment which is available to meet the needs of the hearing, speech, mobility or sight impaired customers. Available as an information tape.

• Public Payphones are fitted with inductive coupler, cards notched for blind but more developments underway.

• Bills available in braille and by tape.

• Zero rating from VAT is confined to equipment designed solely for the use of the disabled.

• Text Users Scheme A call takes much longer for customers who can only use text to communicate. Funded by BT and administered by the RNID those registered receive a 60 per cent rebate on call charges, excluding rental, up to a maximum of £160pa.

• 999 Calls Deaf and speech impaired, especially text users, cannot or have difficulty using 999 service. Some police authorities offer a special number for relaying messages to the emergency services.

Improving accessibility: towards a policy framework

Local authorities have been effectively removed from the ownership and control of infrastructure networks. But the particular problems of urban areas in the 1990s including increasing levels of social polarisation and the conflicts between economic development and environmental quality objectives could see calls for a more integrated approach to the management of the systems. There are a range of institutional linkages between local authorities and utility companies which could be built upon to provide a forum for discussing local levels of access to utility services. Local authorities already liaise with the companies over planning and infrastructure renewal and maintenance while it is quite likely that local members may be represented on the regional committees of utility regulators. Similarly voluntary organisations such as Citizens Advice Bureaux and Age Concern often have to cope with the problems of non-payment of bills, disconnection, deposit charges and disputes with the utilities. Their links with local authorities through housing, social services and environmental health departments could provide the basis of a forum for discussing the problems of access to utilities and developing new policy initiatives. The only statutory link over levels of access is the water companies statutory duty to report all domestic water disconnections to the local environmental health officer.

Local authorities could act as advocates for consumer groups and place pressure on the utilities and the regulators to provide a level of service that reflects the particular social, economic and environmental needs of their city. The key to this role is sufficient understanding of the importance of utility services to different sections of the population and the necessary information and data to monitor the situation. Maps of levels of connection to the telephone network provide the data for lobbying British Telecom and Oftel to increase telephone penetration rates, the setting of development plan policies to encourage public pay-phone provision and encouraging new competitors in the domestic telephony market. Energy data can be used for identifying those areas of the city that should be targeted for the monitoring of fuel poverty and take up of energy efficiency and conservation schemes. The authority could encourage alternative energy suppliers to enter the market while also providing guidance to consumers on the implications of the different energy packages on offer. This type of strategy does not necessarily rely on a set of new powers. The main difficulty is obtaining information on the different aspects of the utilities operations. Attempts could be made to obtain this from the companies, the utility regulators or through pressure put on government to ensure that this information has to be provided on a statutory basis. The data could form a base for identifying consumption by area and different socio-economic groups, setting new environmental and social policy objectives and monitoring the implications of policy initiatives.

Instead of monitoring the operation of markets in infrastructure services and attempting to protect consumers, particularly low income and vulnerable residents, the local authority could seek to become a player in the market. This type of policy could be developed in a number of ways to achieve a range of policy objectives. Local authorities could use their own networks to compete with the existing utilities or even become involved in the provision of new services with the private sector such as the development of cable, CHP/DH and LRT networks. Telephone exchanges could be installed on its own council housing estates to increase levels of telephone provision for low income and vulnerable consumers, create employment in the installation and operation of the system and provide direct services to the local authority and other service agencies. Such initiatives could be developed in partnership with the new cable companies to provide accessible telephony links for low income consumers. In the energy sector local authorities should be able to negotiate energy supply contracts with a number of competing energy supply companies offering heat, electricity and gas or any combination of services. As smart metering technologies become available in the domestic sector local authorities could use their buying power to negotiate a supply package which also includes their council tenants who could benefit from cheaper tariffs or utility led energy efficiency schemes.

If the trends examined here continue it seems to be almost inevitable that local authorities will have to start monitoring local levels of access to infrastructure networks. We can now no longer assume that all households are well connected to water and energy networks. The telephone is already an unaffordable luxury for at least 2 million households and many of those who are connected can only afford a minimal service. If levels of access and quality of service for low income and vulnerable groups do fall new forms of policy intervention will need to be developed.

References

Association of Consumer Research (1991), *Competition and Choice: Telecommunications Policy for the 1990s.*

Boardman, B. (1991a), *Fuel Poverty: from Cold Homes to Homes to Affordable Warmth*, Belhaven Press, London.

Boardman, B. (1991b), *Lessons from ten Cold Years: A Decade of Fuel Poverty*, Policy Discussion Paper, Neighbourhood Energy Action, Newcastle.

DIEL (1991), *Information Pack*, The Advisory Committee on Telecommunications for Disabled and Elderly People, London.

Dobson, J. (1991), "Revolt at the Manor", *Surveyor*, 21st March: 12-13.

Edwards, G. and Cox, G.C. (1982), "The Renewal of Urban Water and Sewerage Systems", in *Planning and the Civil Engineer*, Thomas Telford, London.

Ernst, J. (1991), "The Privatisation of Essential Services in Britain", Paper to VCOSS Statewide Conference on the Future of the Social and Community Services in Victoria, 30th July.

King, M. (1992), *Cold Shouldered*, Winter Action on Cold Homes, London.

Lucy, W.(1981), "Equity and Planning for Local Services", *Journal of the American Planning Association*, Vol. 47, No.4:447-457.

Milne, C. (1989), "Telephones for All?", in *New Consumer Magazine*, September: 20-21.

Milne, C. (1990), Universal Telephone Service in the UK: An Agenda for Policy Research and Action, in *Telecommunications Policy*, October: 365-371.

National Association of Citizens Advice Bureaux (1991), *Paying for Water: NACAB Response to the OFWAT Consultation*, NACAB, London.

National Consumer Council (1989), *In the Absence of Competition: A Consumer View of Public Utilities Regulation*, HMSO.

National Consumer Council (1991a), *Consumer Concerns 1991: Consumer Satisfaction with Public and Local Services*, MORI Survey.

National Consumer Council, (1991b), *Paying for Water: NCC Response to the Ofwat Consultation*, NCC, London.

National Consumer Council, (1991c), *Telecommunications for UK Consumers,* NCC, London.

OFWAT (1990), *Paying for Water: A Time for Decisions, Consultation Paper on Future Charging Policy for Water and Sewerage Services.*

OFWAT (1991a), *Levels of Service Report for the Water Industry of England and Wales 1990/91.*

OFWAT (1991b), *Guidelines on Services for Disabled and Elderly Customers.*

Public Utilities Access Forum (1991), *Terms of Reference.*

Rural Development Commission (1989), *Telecommunications in Rural England*, Rural Research Series Number 2, Economic and Transport Planning Group, report prepared for Oftel and the RDC, London.

Rural Development Commission (1990), *Provision of Basic Utilities in Rural Areas*, Rural Research Series Number 6, RDC, London.

The Independent, (1992) 15th May: 2.

Tinker, A. (1989a), *The Telecommunications Needs of Disabled and Elderly People - An Exploratory Study*, Oftel, London.

Tinker, A. (1989b), "Better than a neighbour: tenants' views of the phone", *Housing*, June: 39-41.

Wicks, M. (1978), *Old and Cold: Hypothermia and Social Policy,* Heinemann.

Chapter 9

Housing design and policy

Introduction

The size and complexity of the housing field limits the scope of this examination to an exploration of the major areas of discrimination and some insights into developing more sensitive practice. The chapter begins with issues of design but then goes onto broader policy issues. While the design of new build and renovated property has become, for some social housing providers, an academic matter as changes in financial resources have reduced new build programmes, all providers have opportunities to evaluate the rules which give housing to some and not to others or which place certain groups of applicants into pigeon holes, for instance, young single people and single parents don't want gardens, all Black people want to live together, and 'couple' means a man and a woman.

Meeting need through sensitive design

Too frequently, when considering housing design in respect of disadvantaged groups, there is a focus on housing for those needing mobility or wheelchair housing as if all other groups of applicants could have their needs met by the 'normal' model, give or take a few rooms. This assumption needs to be challenged.

Not just special needs

The International Year of the Disabled in 1981 saw the introduction of the wheelchair symbol which has proved to be both a breakthrough and a burden. While universally recognised as drawing attention to physical disability it has fused the wheelchair and the disabled together suggesting that the only form of disability is motor impairment. It is not the intention of this section to reiterate the requirements of this group which are set out in the authoritative *Designing for the Disabled* (Goldsmith, 1967) except to draw attention to the constructive attitude of the Dutch to this housing issue.

In 1985 the Dutch Federation of Housing Associations started an experiment on adaptable housing with the aim of developing ordinary housing which could be easily and inexpensively adapted to meet the changing mobility needs of the occupant. This might suggest that these dwellings need to be very large which requires a large initial investment. In fact the Dutch emphasise that the requirement is not for a large dwelling but for one which is spacious enough in certain areas, for example, having a hallway which is wide enough near doors to allow turning but not necessarily wide over the whole length (Nolte, 1991). The philosophy behind the scheme is to eradicate the concept that to be disabled is 'a deviation from the needs of the average tenant' and to replace it with the more holistic idea that disability is simply a variation.

The association of motor impairment with disability has meant that the needs of other groups with different disabilities have not gained the recognition that they deserve.

A design guidance note, to be produced by the Royal National Institute for the Blind in 1993, provides information about the aspects of housing design which need to be considered when thinking of the living requirements of a visually impaired person. These include:

- all doors to be self closing or sliding to avoid the risk of walking into an open door.

- non slip floor surfaces.

- the recessing of possible obstructions such as radiators.

- plenty of power sockets to avoid the risk of trailing flexes.

- a dog run for a guide dog though the percentage of blind people who use a guide dog is small.

- good level of lighting which casts little shadow and is without glare.

- strong colour contrasts e.g door frames, door numbers against doors, in floors with walls (RNIB, 1992).

As a result of care in the community policies more people with profound disabilities are coming out of institutional care and looking for independent or assisted independent living in the community. For such groups there may be a need for dwellings which will allow space for a live in carer or for allocations policies which consider assistance to the disabled person. Habinteg built a scheme for the Muscular Dystrophy Group in Kent which has five flats for people with Muscular Dystrophy and five dwellings for families who have agreed to give a set number of hours help.

Women have been thought of in a stereotypical way in relation to policies towards housing design; that is predominantly as housewives (Roberts, 1992).

The view of women as predominantly unwaged individuals with domestic and child rearing responsibility, who can depend on a male wage, is a long way from being a true picture of British society and yet, in terms of housing design, it still predominates. The truth is that most women, of working age, are in waged work, one third of all marriages end in divorce, three quarters of single parent households are headed by women, women live longer and their longevity means an increasing risk of disability. In addition black women, lesbians, single women, younger disabled women with or without partner and / or children all have needs which may not be adequately met by the conventional house type. Consider a typical house plan:

• how many living spaces does it have? Is there space for individuals to spend time apart engaging in different activities.

• is there space for working at home?

• is there space for more than one person to work in the kitchen?

• is there space to eat in the kitchen as well as a formal eating space?

• is there storage space for a pram? Has the fashion for buggies arisen because of shrinking space standards?

• is it possible to achieve privacy - how many people can hear their neighbours having a row or making love through the wafer thin walls?

Many of these issues concern men as well as women but, in spite of women 's involvement in waged work, women are still more likely to spend more time at home either taking primary responsibility for housework or because they take time out of their careers to raise children. Tom Woolley (forthcoming) states that people have different ideas about their housing from those held by social landlords and private developers. In the social rented sector, women through increased participation in the design process, have had some impact though the caution of funding bodies has stifled more innovative design in this country. The caution of the Housing Corporation is now coupled with lower levels of Housing Association Grant and the push to borrow on the money markets all of which conspires against innovation and increased space standards. The most innovative examples seem to be found in continental Europe:

The idea of shared communal space has been developed extensively in Denmark through the use of a covered street linking terraced houses. Apart from the energy saving aspects of these mini atria, the covered streets provide a point of social contact between neighbours, whatever the weather. [A] scheme at Jystrup, combines common facilities with an internal street to provide safer places for children to play (Woolley, forthcoming).

Other examples from Germany provide space for householders to work from home. Examples from the United States (Franck and Ahrentzen, 1991; Franck forthcoming) examine how a range of dwelling types offering shared spaces and shared support services may benefit women if only as a transitional home offering something more than shelter. Compare this thinking with the often squalid refuges offered to women in this country needing housing and support. Good practice does exist as illustrated below but notice that the work is largely funded by Trusts. Innovation happens because of the commitment of the women involved not the commitment of mainstream funders.

Merseyside Improved Houses identified one of their properties. The group [Amadudu, dedicated to providing a refuge for black women and white women with black children] then raised £40,000 from a variety of Trusts to convert the building. The house has six bedrooms, some with en suite kitchens, and emergency dormitory, a communal kitchen with individual, separate cooking facilities, living room, bathrooms and shower rooms, creche / playroom, and office. Each bedroom is decorated in a different pastel shade, with pine beds, bunk beds, and matching furniture. Time, money and effort has been taken to create a comfortable, safe atmosphere, attention paid to detail like matching bed linen and decent kitchen equipment. Child safe furniture and equipment (Young, 1991).

Design needs of the black community

It is true that in most British cities there is little acknowledgement of the presence of other cultures in the built form. Sheffield City Council (1991), in its UDP, talks of

designs which reflect the ethnic and cultural background of the various groups of people living in Sheffield will be encouraged, where appropriate (BE 3, j).

In the past the black communities have received little attention from providers of new build social housing and have been expected to accept the typical English house. The result has been that many Asian families, in particular, have been unable to consider new build housing as an option because this is often built to suit one type of family - two adults and two children. Since the mid eighties more housing specially designed to meet black needs has sprung up as a result of the Housing Corporation's strategy though it is important to point to Ujima and Asra as two long established associations. The marginalisation of black housing needs leaves many areas, including design, under researched and what is needed is an examination of:

• the design of new build property offered by black associations.

• is there a demand for different design?

- have these preferences been met and if not is this because of cost?

- is there an increase in satisfaction for those living in such dwellings?

Housing policy and practice

The reliance on the market means that those with good income, savings and capital assets prosper, in theory, and those with little or none of these are forced into renting which is generally not a quality choice. Government's lionizing of housing association's should see an increase of quality property under responsible management but a paucity of resources means that the percentage of households living in housing association property remains very small.

In spite of the instability of the market leading to a situation where more than a million British households live in mortgaged property worth less than the loan, there is no sign of any commitment by government to renting in the form of extra resources for housing associations. Political ideology remains a stumbling block to investing more money in local authority renting except as part of a strings attached package such as Housing Action Trust or Estate Action both of which are intended to break up municipal control of housing estates.

British housing policy seems to be in the grip of an Orwellian philosophy which promotes owner occupation above all else irrespective of the suitability of that tenure for certain household groups or of the financial impossibility of ownership for many households. The chapters in section one discussed poverty as a major shared factor among disadvantaged groups. In housing terms the reliance on an ability to pay increases the inequalities suffered by these groups:

- Black people disadvantaged by the education and employment market find themselves in poorly waged work or in self employment on the margins of profitability. Their low level incomes limit their choices. Discrimination in the rented market has, in the past, forced black people into owner occupation (Rex and Moore, 1967) of dubious quality (CRE, 1985) and more recently into rented property of lesser quality (CRE, 1984 & 1989 etc.).

- Disabled people, widely seen as unemployable, are denied an equal education which gives them poor skill and qualification levels. They are further constrained by poor accessibility of work premises. They are reliant on the social rented sector to recognise their housing need and invest in well designed new build or rehabilitation. Substantial cuts in local authority funding and insufficient funding for housing associations means that provision is insufficient and where it exists often perpetuates segregation.

- On retirement the income of elderly people often drops considerably. Increasingly Britain is a nation of home owners and this also applies to the elderly (Department of the Environment, 1986) who are more likely to own a property in a poor state of repair, which lack an inside lavatory.

115

Owner occupation, not necessarily a blessing at any time, may become a terrible burden in old age. In the rented market elderly people may suffer from ageist thinking which confuses housing with care.

• Single women and those partnered by women are less likely to be owner occupiers because of lower earnings and are more likely to have a reduced ability to work because of care responsibilities (Watson, 1986; Sexty, 1990). Women are more numerous in the ranks of the elderly and are more often found among the homeless with or without children and are therefore dependent on the rented sector which may not fully recognise their needs.

This section examines the ways in which current policies and practices may militate against these groups and gives examples of good practice and suggestions for responding more sensitively in spite of lessened resources.

Meeting the housing needs of women

Jane Darke (1989) commenting on how women's housing needs differed from men saw three social differences. Firstly, that women are poorer having lower wages, a greater likelihood of working part rather than full time and both at a time when government places a heavy reliance on the private housing sector and therefore an ability to pay. Secondly, women are more likely to need extra help from their housing because in addition to a job or taking away the possibility of a paid job is the responsibility for children or for a disabled, sick or elderly person. Finally, women's housing needs often arise out of a sudden life event: pregnancy, relationship breakdown, sexual or physical violence. This examination of women and housing looks at these three issues in turn.

Women, poverty and housing costs

At the beginning of the Conservative era, Mrs Thatcher speaking of her Right To Buy proposals, used a female image to convey the benefits of the policy:

> Mothers with small children living in tower blocks, just as anyone else living in tower blocks, will, under a Conservative government now have three options: to carry on renting, to put down an option to purchase the flat within a reasonable time, or to purchase the flat. That seems to me to enlarge the freedom and possibilities available to such people. (Thatcher, 1979).

An examination of any statistics on the take up of Right To Buy (Nationwide Anglia, 1988) reveals that few households in this category are able to enlarge their freedoms. Indeed it can be argued that the operation of the Right To Buy has curtailed choice by decreasing the quantity and quality of stock at a time of increasing female reliance on the rented sector.

While discriminatory practices by building societies have long since been eradicated, rising house prices, fluctuating house prices and a payment system which bears down heavily in the early years of repayment, mean that a single wage needs to be a decent one. Women, as the chapter on employment demonstrates, are often in lower paid jobs or part time work.

Where women do get into owner occupation it is often at the lowest end (Nationwide Anglia, 1988) in unimproved property with a lower standard of amenities.

Various schemes have come forward to ease entry onto the market and some of these have been beneficial to women. Equity sharing has allowed women with equity from a former home, perhaps a house taken on with a relationship, to re-enter owner occupation. If owner occupation has to be the solution then what is needed is even greater flexibility:

- shared ownership with a housing association who will undertake repairs, buy out and sell on for those needing to move quickly.

- staircasing down as well as up for those whose circumstances change such as having a relationship breakdown.

- for an older person, the chance of selling a property onto a responsible landlord who might offer accommodation at a peppercorn rent.

Of course, there is nothing wrong with renting and it can be argued that instead of promoting the dubious benefits of owner occupation to those with marginal resources, there is a pressing need for policies backed with resources to promote renting as a quality not a second rate alternative.

In the mind of government the quality rented market is dominated by housing associations but the mixed funding arrangements coupled with lower levels of HAG, has pushed rents past affordability making many households with waged workers dependent on Housing Benefit. The issue of affordability continues to be debated with various suggestions as to what percentage of income should meet housing costs. An important contribution has been made by Marion Roberts (1991) who has stated that

affordability should be computed on the basis of women's earnings not the now, often outmoded, idea that there is a male wage earner and therefore more likely to be someone earning at or above the decency threshold.

Work done in 1991 by a northern housing association suggested that only those single parents in the higher earning bracket could afford an assured renting property. An article in 'Inside Housing' (November, 1991) said that a housing association, three bedroom house in London would require an income of £20,000 per year to make the rent of £92.96 per week, affordable. If associations are to build for those at lower income levels then there is a need for government to increase the level of subsidy at construction stage. The alternative is to dramatically reduce space standards and realistically the decrease would have to be truly dramatic to have any effect on cost. The practice of buying in package deals from private builders has already led to poorer space standards. It should be remembered that while under occupation is very common in the owner occupied sector it is usual for social rented dwellings to be let to their full capacity making space standards more critical. The only feasible solution, but one which remains unlikely, is for an increased subsidy to housing providers.

Different needs

This issue is dealt with, in part, by the opening section on design but architects and housing managers need to be aware of women's safety needs. It is not enough to consider safety narrowly as an issue which involves allocating a woman, made homeless by domestic violence, to a property out of her partner's reach. How many women, in this situation, are then allocated a property on an estate where vandalism is rife or into a maisonette in a walk up block where stair wells are seldom well lit if at all? Of course, resources play a big part in this. Perhaps the issue is not a lack of awareness of safety needs but that this awareness cannot override the poor general quality of stock and the lack of more suitable property in better areas.

Greater urgency

> Powerlessness is a crucial element in women's relationship with local housing authorities when seeking alternative sources of housing in order to leave an unhappy relationship. Having somewhere to go is probably the single most important in enabling a woman to leave her husband (sic) and in this sense housing policy and practice can make it either possible or impossible for women to leave their husbands. (Morris and Winn, 1990: 126).

The chapter on sexism discussed the poverty of provision for those women trying to leave a violent partner and make a start alone. It is not simply the poor spread of refuges - where do women who live in rural areas go - but the, often, squalid conditions that exist in them. This comes down to resources again but decisions about where money is spent are based on judgements of what, and who are priorities. Frequently the attitude to women fleeing violence is that they are 'sluts and slatterns' who are probably going to go back to their partner so why bother and spend money on them.

Women with children can claim protection under the homeless legislation though the quality of housing they can expect is being undermined by a lack of investment by central government. The position of other groups such as young, childless women is unclear and is a matter for individual authorities to determine. Shelter has found that only 17 per cent of local authorities usually accept young people as homeless (Dibblin, 1991). Preliminary findings from the Housing Corporation's Rooflessness package, funded under the Single Homeless Initiative, highlight some interesting issues which warrant further investigation (Cheeseman, 1992). The research showed that more men than women were helped - only 26 per cent were women - but since the package was aimed at rough sleepers who are more likely to be men, this shows more about the package than about the homeless in general. When asked where they had spent the previous night, only 7 per cent of women had slept rough while 63 per cent had stayed in a hostel: this compares to 31 per cent and 49 per cent of men respectively. The sexual risks to women in sleeping rough may well deter all but the totally desperate from taking this course of action. Over half of the women who were assisted by the Rooflessness package were black, while only 19 per cent of men were black. In analysing age, women were overwhelmingly younger than men - 78 per cent were under 25 years old compared to only 43 per cent of men. Both age and ethnicity need to be further examined to see why young black women are increasingly to be found without shelter. Is this because of increasingly restrictive housing policies in urban centres? Is it racism which denies them temporary shelter? Is it sexual and racial harassment in private and public renting forcing these women out?

Meeting the housing needs of gay men and lesbians

Lucy Wilkinson (1992), in her analysis of questionnaires sent to London and metropolitan housing authorities, revealed that the overall performance of authorities in responding to the housing needs of gay man and lesbians was poor. Those which included lesbians and gay men in their equal opportunities policies performed well on a few issues but their overall performance was not much better than other authorities suggesting that equal opportunities policies are not necessarily put into practice nor fully thought out when they are.

Every allocation system which was examined discriminated against gay men and lesbians, in some way, though eighty per cent of officers who completed the questionnaire believed that their system was fair. The two main problems which came to light in Wilkinson's research was firstly, the widespread use of language that excluded lesbian or gay households such as 'man and wife or living as man and wife' and secondly, points systems which favoured certain household types, generally married couples. In their interpretation of the Code of Guidance on homelessness, some authorities were restrictive to the detriment of lesbian or gay applicants. For example, some did not count violence and harassment on the grounds of sexuality as reason for becoming homeless, thus placing lesbians and gay men on a lower footing than women fleeing violent men, women who are sexually harassed or black men and women harassed and attacked because of their colour.

Only four authorities included anti-lesbian or gay harassment as a specific breach of the tenancy agreement. Those that did had a higher rate of reported incidents suggesting that the presence of such a clause encourages people to report incidents with some confidence that they will be treated with seriousness and sensitivity. Only twenty nine percent of authorities gave all households equal rights in granting joint tenancies or tenancies after the death of the tenant.

In the face of such discrimination one development would be for lesbians and gay men to organise their own housing. Local authorities could use their 'enabling role' to facilitate this though only seventeen per cent of authorities were involved in any gay or lesbian housing project. A further step foward would be to recognise the part that staff training could play in creating awareness of gay and lesbian issues in general and housing in particular.

From her study Lucy Wilkinson produces a set of recommendations which are reproduced below with her permission.

Recommendations

• Local authorities should review their allocation policies to check that they do not discriminate against lesbians and gay men in particular they should look at:
  - language used (e.g to define relationships between household members).
  - whether the points / allocations system unjustifiably favours certain household types, such as married couples compared to other couples including points awarded for relationship breakdown and separated households.
  - whether 'reasonable offer' policies take the needs of lesbians and gay men, regarding safety, into account.

• Local authorities should look at positive action measures to reverse discrimination in access to housing, for example by:
  - awarding lesbians and gay men points if they are suffering harassment, are isolated from the lesbian or gay community or are living with relatives who are unhappy about their sexuality.
  - providing encouragement to lesbians and gay men to apply for housing.
  - providing training for staff involved in the allocations procedure.
  - monitoring allocations on the basis of sexuality, though recognising the limits to this as many lesbians and gay men will be unwilling to 'come out' on an application form.

• Local authorities should try to meet the needs of homeless lesbians and gay men by:
  - ensuring that anti-lesbian or gay violence is counted as a reason for homelessness.
  - looking at sexuality when considering if someone is 'vulnerable' and therefore in priority need.
  - not assuming that reconciliation with family is the best way of rehousing young homeless lesbians and gay men.
  - recognising the importance of community and a variety of household structures when assessing whether a lesbian or gay man has a local connection with the borough.
  - providing more funding and help with development for temporary accommodation designed to meet the needs of homeless lesbians and gay men.
  - liaising with the Department of the Environment to get the above points written onto the Code of Guidance on homelessness.

• Local authorities should ensure that lesbians and gay men have equal rights to heterosexuals in terms of getting joint tenancies and succession or granting of tenancies after the death of the tenant. Family units should be self defined, so the above rights apply not only to couples but to any people who live together as a household.

• Local authorities should recognise that lesbians and gay men are vulnerable to harassment on the grounds of sexuality and also may be particularly vulnerable to other forms of harassment such as racial harassment and harassment of people with disabilities. In response, they should:

- include anti-lesbian or gay harassment as a specific breach of the tenancy agreement to encourage reporting and to raise awareness of the issue amongst officers and potential perpetrators.

- draw up clear procedures for dealing with anti-lesbian or gay harassment, including the five elements listed below.

- support for the person being harassed (including private tenants)

- provision of emergency, temporary accommodation, if required.

- action against perpetrators, if desired by the accommodation suffering harassment.

- transfer, as a last resort.

- strict confidentiality.

• Local authorities should look at staff training to ensure that staff are aware of issues affecting lesbians and gay men. They should bear in mind:

- the need for compulsory training, so that all receive it.

- the feelings of lesbian and gay staff who may be participating.

- incorporating lesbian and gay case studies into existing training.

- that the experiences of all lesbians and gay men should be represented, for example Black lesbians and gay men, elderly lesbians and gay men in sheltered accommodation.

- incorporating lesbian and gay issues into training carried out for other groups, eg tenants' groups.

• Local authorities should encourage the development of lesbian and gay housing projects, which aim to redress previous discrimination, through:

- providing funding. properties and. other forms of support such as expertise, to co-ops, housing associations or temporary accommodation projects.

- recognising the needs of different groups of lesbians and gay men by providing support for example, to women-only projects, those run by Black lesbians and gay men and those providing housing for lesbians and gay men who are elderly or have disabilities.

Housing for disabled people

Did you move here because of your health problem / disability? (OPCS in Oliver, 1990).

What inadequacies in your housing caused you to move here? (Oliver, 1990).

'Inadequacy' is a word that readily comes to mind when considering housing for people with disabilities. Research done by Jenny Morris for Shelter (1990) revealed that local authorities were largely ignorant of the disabled people in their borough and their demands for housing. Furthermore, most had poor records detailing which properties had been adapted and how they had been adapted.

In 1989, completions of adapted dwellings fell to 1,200 from 4,300 in 1981 (Inside Housing, 1991). Both figures relate to local authority and housing association provision. The number of houses designed to full wheelchair standard in this country is about 30,000 compared to some 80,000 wheelchair users. For a group of people so highly dependent on the social rented sector, this picture can only be a calamity.

The Housing Corporation has committed itself to a strategy for 'special needs' and some associations have increased their work in this area, but provision is poor and the financial situation is not conducive to the building of affordable wheelchair units. As the section on design suggested, the majority of disabled people don't need this level of provision. Their needs can be met by mobility housing with various adaptations to meet specific requirements. Moreover, there are examples of disabled people coming together to fight for better provision. One such example is the efforts made in 1991 by the North Tyneside Disability Group. This small group of people comprising of wheelchair users, people with visual impairment and those with mobility difficulties researched the housing need of disabled people, visited other schemes up and down the country to determine appropriate models and finally having gained the commitment of Habinteg Housing Association, made a convincing presentation to the local authority. While the scheme has yet to begin on site, it illustrates disabled people carrying their own fight and empowering themselves.

There are also examples of responsive organisations with a client centred approach but with six million disabled people in this country there is a need for some national network of such bodies working in partnership with statutory and voluntary agencies.

[The Disabled Person's Housing Service] is an agency of Walbrook Housing Association in Derby. Formed in 1985 in response to requests from disabled people, it has grown by meeting their needs for a single agency, a one-stop shop, where they can share their housing problems, receive sound advice and factual input and get practical help. Almost half of those who approach the DPHS want housing or rehousing; the rest are seeking adaptations for their existing homes, or advice, or the support of an agency which understands housing and cares about people. The DPHS's first response is always the same: to listen carefully (Kendall, 1991).

Those in their own homes face the difficulties of financing adaptation. The changes to the grant regime which were introduced in 1989 promised less complexity but this has been wholly overturned by the means test which now applies to grant applications. Department of Environment figures for the period July 1990 to March 1991 indicate that while 21,000 people made enquiries about the disabled facilities grant, only 4,000 made it to grant approval stage. The Royal Association for Disability and Rehabilitation [RADAR] (1992) criticises the means test for failing to take into account

122

mortgage repayments and, the extra costs involved in being a disabled person, which might mean special diet, extra heating, transport, laundry costs, the purchase of care. While apparently making finance available for keeping disabled people in the community and improving their quality of life, the grant regime is an opportunity for only a small group leaving others to consider the real possibility of going into care because their living environment is unsuitable or even dangerous.

[Rachel Todd was] disabled some years ago by an industrial injury for which she received a lump sum in compensation, Ms Todd uses the income from the invested lump sum to pay for personal care. But her savings disqualify her from receiving a grant for adaptations to her home, which she now needs because her disability is increasing as she grows older. Ms Todd has the impossible choice of using her savings to adapt her home to make it livable, or continuing to pay for the cost of personal care, without which she could not carry on living at home. (Morris, 1991)

Government is currently examining the means test with a view to improving the targeting on poorer households. It remains to be seen whether review will create opportunity for disabled people.

Housing policies for older people

To examine housing for the elderly is to uncover not so much a lack of housing policy as a confusion of policy. While about forty per cent of the elderly are owner occupiers this leaves a majority without collateral to provide for their housing needs in the market place. A large percentage of the owner occupiers still have the problem of raisi sufficient capital to purchase a more suitable dwelling or a flat in private sheltered housing. To move from owner occupation to a rented dwelling is to be obliged to pay the unrebated rent because of capital limits. The change to mixed funding schemes has caused the rents of sheltered housing units to rise considerably. Coupled with severe tapers in housing benefit, this has resulted in making them unaffordable to even those elderly who have modest occupational pensions and no accumulated capital. Housing associations, often, have to work through a substantial waiting list of those elderly people in housing need before finding someone who can afford the rent without hardship.

Local authorities ability to build new sheltered housing schemes has been halted while the Housing Corporation now allocate some 10 per cent of funds to sheltered housing as opposed to 30 per cent of recent years (Fletcher, 1992). At the same time elderly people may apply for sheltered housing though their needs may be well met by a small flat or bungalow with central heating and security from a door locking system and / or a call alarm scheme. Needless to say these are being built in even smaller numbers though local authorities such as Newcastle MBC have long had a policy of converting tower blocks into quasi sheltered housing.

For many elderly people the choice is simply one of staying put. This may be their wish or it may arise from lack of alternatives. Staying put is government's preferred option in line with community care policies but is weakened by the cuts in domiciliary services made by social services departments to avoid charge capping. This may lead some elderly people to enter residential care which ironically has been bolstered by revenue contributions from the Department of Social Security. These have encouraged housing associations also to build residential care. Alternatives to staying put may arise not from any examination of housing need among the elderly but from a commercial need to maximise revenue support from government. Accordingly recent studies suggest that a third of those in residential care don't need to be there and are in danger of losing their independence and individuality as a result (Harbert, 1992).

Sheltered housing

While the concept of level and accessible housing for older people has been around since the immediate post war with the building of small flats and grouped bungalow schemes the term 'sheltered housing' conjures up the vision of a block dwelling with flats and communal facilities. This particular form of sheltered housing, known as category two, was established by the DoE circular 82/69 which set out space and amenity standards.

The circular talks of category two being aimed at the 'less active elderly' though this is a vague concept. Furthermore it became quickly established that the role of the warden was to be a 'good neighbour' though with the proviso that the things that a good neighbour would help with such as changing a lightbulb, getting in a few groceries, filling a prescription were not within a warden's remit. The traditional image of the warden has been of a good natured and untrained Mrs Cannybody who can run a coffee morning and call at Bingo. The vague role of the warden had led to the odd practice of letting flats in schemes to people who don't need the facilities of a warden, a call alarm scheme, the lounge etc in an effort not to burden the warden with too many frail people (Clapham and Munro, 1988).

The field of housing is seldom scrutinised for its attitudes to older people. Yet the dramatic expansion of sheltered housing has probably contributed to the view of this age group being especially dependent. The very words "sheltered housing" conjure up an image of elderly people who need protection (Marshall, 1990).

The last few years have seen a re-evaluation of sheltered housing in all it aspects and a new framework has emerged:

• Because of dwindling opportunities to add to the stock and increased demand by frailer and older people, sheltered housing is seen as a scarce resource. This has led to better targeting with more stringent examination of social as well as housing need and allocations made jointly with social workers.

• The need to maximise the resources afforded by sheltered housing. A visit to most schemes will reveal that the communal lounge is used infrequently during the day. This is happening while community groups have a more difficult search for premises. There is no reason why the lounge cannot be used by other groups particularly those aimed at older

124

people or those whose activities or talks would keep the sheltered tenants alive to the concerns of the wider community.

• The introduction of care packages for sheltered housing tenants with needs met in their flats by either social services support or support workers employed by the housing association. Anchor Housing Association have such a scheme which covers the needs of their six hundred tenants in Newcastle upon Tyne. The concept is that services flow to an individual as needed and are increased or withdrawn as necessary.

• The warden is there to evaluate need and to act as a co-ordinator of care, perhaps providing short term care where necessary.

• The building of sheltered housing for black elderly people recognises the unmet needs of this group and empowers black citizens by having them define their own needs. How these schemes will operate and what they aim to offer to whom is a matter for the association and the community.

• The establishment of extra care, or category 2 1/2, for frailer people.This offers a greater degree of independence than residential care but with some of the services associated with this sector such as the provision of cooked meals by a central kitchen.

There are problems, of course. Local authorities, with cuts in social services spending, may find it difficult to make the necessary services available and there is always the argument that services should go to those out in the community rather than those privileged to be in sheltered housing. In addition, there is the pressure to allocate to older people in local authority family dwellings to release property for homeless families.

The targeting of sheltered housing to frailer people has led to more positive attitudes to the larger group of elderly, seeing them as individuals who are more likely to continue living in their own accommodation. The arguments about bringing in varying levels of care can apply to those who stay put in their own home.

Staying put

There are now more than 140 Care and Repair or Staying Put schemes operating in Britain aimed at elderly owner occupiers who want to remain in their own homes and need counselling and advice as to what repair works could be carried out and who might fund them. A report from Anchor looking at those who had work done in the early days of their schemes showed a continued high level of satisfaction and 79 per cent still living in their home.

An area which has received little attention is the choices available to elderly black owner occupiers. Previous research indicated that many black, particularly Asian, households purchased low cost, poor quality inner city dwellings. The renewal policies of the late 60s and early 70s prevented those with high repayament costs taking out grants which needed topping up with loans. It is also acknowledged that, among the black community, there is a greater incidence of poor health and disability often linked to having worked in heavy industry. The fusion of these factors must mean that there are elderly and disabled black citizens whose housing is unsuitable but who are unaware of the availability of grant aid such as the new Disabled Facilities Grant or of assistance from financial institutions. A target for existing schemes must be to reach out to the black community with translated literature, with workers who can communicate with the various communities and a commitment to improving the living conditions for these individuals. Given the poor spread of black sheltered housing schemes and the low take up of residential care by black elderly people there is a greater possibility of a black person continuing to live in their home no matter how unsuitable it is. It is important that a multi racial Britain gives a commitment to black as well as white elderly owner occupiers.

Housing needs of the black community

While data from the 1991 census is awaited, it may well show that more black citizens are living in local authority dwellings. This could be seen as a step forward; a sign of discrimination being eradicated and past barriers to access coming down. It could mean no progress at all. The residualisation of the public sector has resulted in council housing being a sector for those whose problems are not necessarily encompassed by housing need: the homeless, individuals coming through community care programmes, the young and impoverished, the old and impoverished, single parents, the state dependent, disabled person. The issue appears to be not access but access to quality. For access to quality in the rented sector read access to housing association property.

The housing association movement

In May 1983 the National Federation of Housing Associations (NFHA) in reviewing the impact of its 1982 report 'Race and Housing' revealed some interesting gaps in perception between providers and the black communities. Many associations had reviewed their allocations and lettings policies to eradicate bias, with seventy two per cent of London association having done so leading the report to conclude that there was 'a sensitivity to the issue of race which is likely to be found in few other public or private organisations' (NFHA, 1987: 8). The black community's image of the associations was very different. Through questionnaires and meetings with black groups involved in housing issues, the NFHA determined that associations were seen as insensitive to the needs of black people. Within the often predominantly black or multi cultural areas in which associations worked, the communities had no control and little influence over what the associations did. The associations which took part insisted that they had tried many avenues of contact such as advertising their existence and aims on Asian language radio programmes, articles in Asian newspapers and recruiting Asian staff. However, the black communities stated that the associations were inaccessible.

An example of the gap is illustrated by Leicester where associations have been very active in rehabilitating properties in black areas. Housing associations saw themselves as improving the area but the black communities saw this as displacement of black tenants to benefit incoming whites. It is clear that many landlords used various means to get rid of their black tenants in order to sell their property with vacant possession to the associations. Communication channels exist but it is clear that the parties have failed to talk in terms that the other has fully understood.

Since 1983, evidence has come forward to suggest that too many housing associations have achieved very little in terms of race equality (Julienne, 1990):

- 17% of associations appeared not to ensure equality of opportunity in terms of access to their housing, and a further 30% were only adequate.

- Comparatively few associations (7%) were found to take no steps to avoid discrimination, but over 20% did not have clear policies and targets, or failed to monitor their own performance or take positive action.

- 22% of associations did not adequately implement a "fair housing programme" using available good practice guidance, and a further 33% only adequately.

- 21% of associations did not adequately set measurable targets, with the aim of increasing housing provision for black and other minority ethnic people, or implement action plans for achieving change against those targets.

- 19% of associations are a cause for concern, or worse, in adopting policies and procedures on equal treatment, positive action and the elimination of racial discrimination. A further 30% were only adequate.

Findings such as these have been a spur to the development of the black housing association movement aided by the Housing Corporation's five year strategy. This aims to increase rented opportunities for black people; to increase black control over housing and to promote the role of black led associations in meeting black housing needs. In January 1990 there were 83 black associations registered with the NFHA, most of which had been started under the five year programme (NFHA, 1990). While this can be seen as a great step forward it is imperative that the Housing Corporation continues to monitor the performance of all housing associations on the issue of race equality in housing provision, housing access and employment. The growth of black associations must not be seen as an excuse for others to slacken their commitment. Given the greater size of many mainstream bodies and therefore the greater power to do good, there is increased responsibility to take action.

It remains regrettable that the push from the black communities and from the Housing Corporation comes at a time when capital funding regimes militate against the building of new properties which may need to be larger for extended families or to incorporate measures to combat harassment. The ability of a small association with low or no existing asset base to build quality housing to meet different needs at affordable rents has been severely damaged by reduction in Housing Association Grant and new reliance on market loans. Added to this is the issue of land scarcity in some areas and land prices which all serve to make new build unaffordable particularly to black households whose income levels are generally lower than white.

The pressure to produce "value for money" is defined ... in terms of the greatest number of units for a fixed pot of money ... Type and quality ... lose out in the process. This will disadvantage many black and ethnic minority people, who can then only be housed well away from their community roots and support networks. Safety and security, in terms of racial harassment and victimisation, are not issues in the "value for money" debate (Harrison, 1992).

While new build is an important psychological element of any housing programme dedicated to redressing a historical backlog of inequality it remains true that concentration of the black community in the inner city coupled with the land shortage there may result in new build being a distance from cultural support. This may be particularly dislocating to elderly people allocated flats in new build sheltered housing. The Housing Corporation have recognised the problem and have encouraged mainstream associations to make stock transfers to black associations.

Occupants of an Anchor Housing Association scheme in Bradford voted overwhelmingly in favour of the transfer of their homes to Asian association Manningham... Half of the tenants are white. The freehold of the £770,000 scheme, Jervaulx Court, will now transfer to Manningham which has been managing it since 1990. Anchor which built the scheme for Asian elderly people in 1988, identified the scheme as suitable for stock transfer (Inside Housing, 1992).

The change in housing association finance has ended the almost open ended financial commitment from the Housing Corporation which in turn has caused a shift out of rehabilitation work. If this work is not to be left entirely to the private sector there is a need for prioritised funding for inner city rehabilitation to eradicate the bias of the new regime against black housing needs.

The problems do not lie solely with capital funding, there is also a need for increased revenue support for associations particularly in the start up stages when wages and office rentals have to be paid though there is no income. Harrison (1992) details the workings of the Charitable Trust of Housing Associations in West Yorkshire. Mainstream associations agree to make contributions to this trust which then makes grants and loans to black led local associations. While sustaining new bodies, this approach is dependent on voluntary agreements by mainstream committees of management and does not ensure guaranteed support. The Housing Corporation needs to re-examine its procedures and processes which, do not necessarily ensure financial survival for the new associations which it seems eager to promote.

128

Owner occupation

The home ownership of Asians is associated with neither gentrification nor suburbanization but with poverty of choice leading to the purchase of low cost, low quality properties in run down environments (Rex and Moore, 1967; Karn et al, 1985). Rex and Tomlinson (1979) and Brown (1984) have demonstrated that the grant regimes instituted under the General Improvement Area programmes and under Housing Action Areas brought little benefit to this group of owners in spite of their eligibility. There are a number of possible explanations. Firstly, that high interest, non building society loans created an inability to take up the necessary top up loan to the grant. Secondly, that part of the work needed may have been ineligible for grant and therefore fell to the owner to fund. Thirdly, that poor communication between local authorities and communities meant that black communities were not involved in decision making. Since then, a new grant regime, has been introduced which hinges on means testing as a condition of eligibility for grant. Research is needed to determine whether the black community is applying and whether there is a greater success rate though again it is important to discover the reasons. Ethnic monitoring is important in all stages of the process to determine who applies and who is successful and, in respect of area programmes, which properties and which occupants are targeted first. Ratcliffe (1992: 398) has pointed out the real danger to meeting black housing needs from financial imperatives which demand a high through-put of property militating against the common sense worst first approach.

Conclusions

An examination of housing policy sees the closing of more doors than are opened. The new reliance on the markets means fewer opportunities for those in housing need, with no or few financial resources, to gain access to quality housing. Increasingly many groups are seeing their only choice as owner occupation though this may mean the purchase of a poor quality dwelling with all the attendant responsibilities for repair and maintenance. For others dependent on social landlords there is a choice between the increasingly poor quality of the local authority or the better quality but less available and less affordable housing association dwellings. For all groups, the old, the disabled, the black citizen, single and lesbian women and for gay men the housing future remains bleak without government commitment to a right to rent and greater financial underpinning of the rented sector.

References

Brown, C. (1984), *Black and White Britain*, Heinemann, London.

Cheeseman, P. (1992), "Monitoring the Rooflessness Package in London, February - September 1991", *Homelessness Statistics*, Papers from the seminar of the Statistics Users' Council, 16th December 1991, IMAC Research, Esher.

Clapham, D. and Munro, M. (1988), "Sheltered Housing - not just for those who need it", *Housing*, November: 20-21.

Commission for Racial Equality (1984), *Race and Council Housing in Hackney*, Report of Formal Investigation, CRE Publications, London.

Commission for Racial Equality (1985), *Race and Mortgage Lending:Formal Investigation of Mortgage Lending in Rochdale*, CRE Publications, London.

Commission for Racial Equality (1989), *Racial Discrimination in Liverpool City Council: report of formal investigation into the Housing Department*, CRE Publications, London.

Darke, J. (1989), "Problem without a name", *Roof*, March and April: 31.

Department of the Environment, (1987), *English House Condition Survey 1986*, HMSO, London.

Dibblin, J. (1991), *Wherever I lay my Hat - Young Women and Homelessness*, Shelter, London.

Fletcher, P. (1992), "Housing Policies for Older People", paper to the Institute of Housing National Conference, June.

Franck, K. and Ahrentzen, S. (1991), *New Households, New Housing*, Van Nostrand Reinhold, New York.

Franck, K. (forthcoming), "Women and new initatives in Housing Design in the United States" in Gilroy, R and Woods, R.(eds), *Housing Women*, Routledge, London.

Goldsmith, S. (1967), *Designing for the Disabled*, RIBA, London.

Harbert, W. (1992), Housing Policies for Older People, paper to the Institute of Housing National Conference, June.

Harrison, M. (1992), "Housing associations response to the needs of minority ethnic communities", *Findings*, Joseph Rowntree Foundation, March.

Housing Development Directorate (1974), *Mobility Housing*, Occasional Paper 2/74, HMSO, London.

Housing Development Directorate (1975), *Wheelchair Housing*, Occasional Paper 2/75, HMSO, London.

Inside Housing (1991), "Grant rate cut next year will make rents unaffordable, say association", 1st November.

Inside Housing (1991),"A right to say what we need and get it", 13th December.

Inside Housing (1992), "Black association gets first transfer of tenanted homes", 28th February.

130

Julienne, L. (1990), "Monitoring H.A.s on race equality issues", *Black Housing*, November/ December.

Karn, V. & Kemeny, J. & Wiliams, P. (1985), *Home Ownership in the Inner City*, Salvation or Despair, Gower, Aldershot.

Kendall, R. (1991), "Ask us what we want!", *Community Network*, Autumn: 7 - 8.

Marshall, M. (1990), "Proud to be Old" in (ed) McEwen, E. *Age: The Unrecognised Discrimination*, Age Concern, London.

Ministry of Housing and Local Government and the Welsh Office (1969), *Housing Standards and Costs. Accommodation Specially Designed For Older People*, HMSO, London.

Morris, J. and Winn, M. (1990), *Housing and Social Inequality*, Hilary Shipman, London.

Morris, J. (1990), *Our Homes, Our Rights*, Shelter, London.

Morris, J. (1991), "Adding injustice to disability", *Inside Housing*, 18th October.

National Federation of Housing Associations (1987), *Race - Still a cause for concern*, NFHA, London.

National Federation of Housing Associations (1990), *Supporting Black Housing Associations*, NFHA, London.

Nationwide Anglia Building Society (1988), "Lending to Women".

Nolte, E. (1991), "Providing Adaptable Housing - The Dutch Experience", Institute of Housing National Conference, June.

Ratcliffe, P. (1992), "Renewal, regeneration and 'race': Issues in urban policy", *New Community*, vol 18, no3, April: 387-400.

Rex, J. and Moore, R. (1967), *Race, Community and Conflict*, Oxford University Press, London.

Rex, J. and Tomlinson, S. (1979), *Colonial Immigrants in a British City*, Routledge and Kegan Paul, London..

Roberts, M. (1992),"Women: The Silent Majority", in Darke, J. (ed), *The Roof Over Your Head*, Spokesman Books, Nottingham.

Roberts, M. (1991), *Living in a Man made world: Gender Assumptions in Modern Housing Design*, Routledge, London.

Royal Association for Disability and Rehabilitation (1992), "The disabled facilities grant", RADAR, London.

Royal National Institute for the Blind (1992), Promotional leaflet for RNIB Housing Service.

Sexty, C. (1990), *Women Losing Out*, Shelter, London.

Sheffield City Council (1991), Draft Unitary Development Plan.

Thatcher, M. (1979), House of Commons Parliamentary Debate, vol 967, session 1979-1980, c. 1223.

Watson, S. (1986), "The Marginalisation of non-family Households in Britain", *International Journal of Urban and Regional Research*, vol 10, no 2, March: 8-28.

Wilkinson, L. (1992) "The Housing Needs of Lesbians and Gay men - The Response of Local Authorities. Dissertation for the Post Graduate Diploma in Housing Policy and Management, University of Newcastle upon Tyne and Newcastle Polytechnic.

Woolley, T. (forthcoming),"New Initiatives in Housing Design in Europe" in Gilroy, R. and Woods, R.(eds), *Housing Women*, Routledge, London.

Young, A. (1991), "Amadudu - Refuge for Black Women", *Black Housing*, vol. 7, no 3, April: 12-13.

Chapter 10

Employment

In a society where access to services and facilities of quality is determined more and more by ability to pay it becomes increasingly important not only that you have a job but that it pays sufficient to lift you out of the poverty trap and into the arena of choice. A job supplies income and also status, it determines where you live, it may give assistance with a home loan or bridging loan, legal fees on moving, it may supply a car for work or give interest free loans for season tickets, health care insurance, free telephone calls, luncheon vouchers or subsidised canteens. A job then is more than a means of earning a crust; it offers other rewards as well as psychologically offering a person a means of structuring their time, gaining status and finding identity. How many of us when asked who we are respond with name and occupation?

It is clear that employment opportunities are not distributed equally: decision makers and those in prestige jobs are more likely to be white, male and able bodied. This section examines the world of work considering firstly the present position of disadvantaged groups and then moving on to explore the barriers to entry and advancement before setting out some examples and strategies for breaking down these barriers.

A further issue for all service providers dedicated to quality service for all is that employment of women, of black people, of disabled people will or should sensitize the service to those groups. The operative word is 'should:' to employ a wide range of people but to employ them in the lowest jobs changes nothing. To make change such people must be in some position of authority: this is rarely the case. This chapter examines why.

The present position

Women

Webster (in Stone, 1988) discussing the nature of women's employment picked out four characteristics of women in work.

A concentration in 'women's services'

In 1984 when Sheffield City Council was analysing its local authority services it discovered that women employees were concentrated in a few departments: Education, Libraries and Social Services where they made up the great majority of both manual and administrative workers. Isabella Stone's study (1988) revealed a similar pattern for other local authorities suggesting that while local authorities are large employers of women, the work that they do may be fulfilling traditional female roles of clerical assistant, librarians, care workers, cleaners and catering staff.

A concentration in part time jobs

A recent household survey undertaken in the West End City Challenge are in Newcastle (University of Newcastle upon Tyne, 1992) revealed a typical employment pattern for women. They were only slightly less likely than men to be in work (24.3 per cent as opposed to 26.6 per cent) but much more likely to be working part time than men (10.9 per cent compared to only 2.7 per cent). The Sheffield study (Stone, 1988) revealed that 84 per cent of the city's manual grades were women part time workers. The nature of part time work has changed in the last few years. The old image of it being manual or low skilled work has altered because of the increase in job sharing for women at all levels including senior professionals. This is an issue to which we will return later in this chapter but for the moment consider the dilemma faced by a woman who needs to work but only wants to work limited hours to fit with caring responsibilities. By abandoning full time work a woman may lose many employment rights such as redundancy payment, protection from unfair dismissal and for some the right to maternity leave. There is a need for a change of employment legislation to ensure that those who take part time work are not disadvantaged and treated as marginal.

Concentration in low paid jobs

The concentration of women in part time and in manual or administrative means that women are often in low paid jobs. The issue of manual work is interesting because men in manual trades are likely to have the chance of overtime and of bonus payments to their flat rate wage. These customs and practices have traditionally been part of the manual work done by men but are not part of women's manual trades. Cynically we might say that women are not expected to work overtime but should be getting home to do their man's dinner! For many households the woman's wage is the only wage but unlike men there is little possibility of gaining more than the basic.

Concentration in lower status jobs

In 1986 Pat Niner and Christine Davies undertook a survey on behalf of the Institute of Housing which revealed the following information:

- almost half of the Local Authority workers were women

- 66 per cent of those on scales 1-3 were women

- 20 per cent of those on senior grades were women

- 13 per cent of those on principal grades were women

- 5 per cent of Chief Housing Officers were women.

This completed the jigsaw picture started by the National Federation of Housing Associations (NFHA) survey undertaken in 1985 which showed that 62 per cent of housing association employees were women. In spite of only making up 38 per cent of workers, there were three times as many male managers and twice as many male professional staff. In terms of income only 28 women as opposed to 224 men were in the highest income bands while at the lowest end of the wage scale there were almost five times as many women as men.

It would be pleasing to see this as representing 'the bad old days' but what of the study of women chief housing officers reported in ROOF (1990). There are now eleven women in Chief Officer posts which is far below the 5 per cent level reported in 1986. Far from making progress women appear to be losing ground. The problems are not unique to housing.

Clara Greed's (1990) work on women in surveying found that they made up only 4.8 per cent of the profession, while in planning:.

> Female planners are found in very small numbers in both the private and public sectors. Where there are women they tend to be found in the lower levels of the staff hierarchy, rarely reaching the level of Principal Officer, in Local authorities or Senior Partners in private consultancies (Collett, Ogden and Hesmondhaugh, 1989).

Research from the United States reveals that women still lag behind men in planning jobs and at the same level can expect to be earning less. Women could expect to earn $1,600 less than a man; a man from a minority group is earning $2,000 less than a white man while a woman from a minority group could be nearly $4000 less than a white man. (Lewis, 1991). The reason we need to look carefully at the United States is that there has been long established anti discrimination legislation with considerably higher financial penalties in a nation more used to taking legal action. In spite of all this women and particularly black women are not reaching the same levels as white men.

In local authorities as a whole there were, in 1988, only 50 women chief officers and only 4 chief executives. This is not a phenomenon peculiar to local government. A 1991 Guardian article revealed that while medical school admissions are running at 50/50 for men and women, only 15 per cent of consultants are women while in the specialism of surgery only 3 per cent of consultants are women and in surgery as a whole there are less than 1 per cent of women general surgeons (Mihill, 1991).

On October 28th 1991 John Major launched the Operation 2000 scheme to encourage top companies to set out equal opportunities goals. The fact that such a campaign is necessary some sixteen years after the passing of the Sex Discrimination Act is an indication of the priority given to equal opportunities and to women's issues in particular. An examination of central government practice reveals the same lack of commitment.

Women in the Civil Service

	MEN	WOMEN
Permanent secretaries	100%	0%
Deputy/Under secretaries	93%	7%

Top Posts (actual figures)

Cabinet Office	16	1
Treasury	41	5
Inland Revenue	26	0
Employment	31	2
Defence	75	1
Scottish Office	36	1

(Source: The Journal, 1991, October 29th)

Studies in all employment sectors reveal not only horizontal segregation where women are pinned at the bottom of the pile but also vertical segregation that is some areas of work are almost exclusively male. The NFHA survey (1985) showed that certain functions such as development had very few women and those tended to be in clerical support positions.

Black people

The unemployment rate in 1981 for Sheffield stood at 14% but within the 7 Wards with a high black population the unemployment rate for the black population was 24% compared to 18% for the white population.

Unemployment amongst young people (16-24 year olds) is much higher and again with a disparity between the black and white

Young people, 34% for black men compared to 25% for white men. The greater corresponding figures for women are 30% and 16% i.e. an even greater disparity.

It is also an established fact that unemployment amongst black people rises much faster than for whites during a recession partly because of the types of jobs done by black people and partly because of racial discrimination and racism. Thus between 1973 and 1980 total national unemployment doubled whilst black unemployment quadrupled. It is

136

reasonable to assume therefore that the situation in Sheffield will have deteriorated considerably for the black population since 1981. Indeed talking to community representatives it is not uncommon to hear them talk of 80-90% unemployment rates amongst their particular community (Sheffield City Council, 1989).

While this extract refers to Sheffield a few strokes of Tippex would make this a picture applicable to many British urban centres.

It is apparent that in spite of legislation, the efforts of trade unions and some dedicated employers, black people are still doing badly in the employment market (Jenkins, 1986). A study in Manchester (Freathy, 1991) demonstrated that black school leavers experienced problems in gaining access to employer led YTS and were often forced to take up places on premium schemes which are much less likely to lead to permanent jobs. These schemes were initially intended for young people with learning difficulties and other special needs so young black people, on such a scheme, have not only less chance of getting a job but run the risk of being labelled as 'problems'.

The thing is you put people on training but there's no jobs at the end. There's nothing at the end, you don't even get a piece of paper (Views of the Black community in University of Newcastle upon Tyne, 1992).

It is difficult to speak with much accuracy of the position of black people as employees of local authorities because few carry out ethnic monitoring of their staff. What figures are available show a picture of under recruitment: Nottingham has a workforce which is 3 per cent black compared to a population which is 12 per cent black. The figures for Sheffield are 1 per cent and 4.5 per cent respectively though the latter figure excludes teachers; while the London Borough of Camden which might be expected to exhibit greater equality has a workforce which is 20 per cent black compared to 30 per cent of the population.

Carving out the position of black women is less easy but the little evidence available suggests that they are pinned at the bottom in low status jobs. Stone's study for the Equal Opportunities Commission (1988) revealed that, of the black women who worked for Sheffield City Council, 40 per cent worked for Social Services with more than two thirds of these in catering or care work. Only four black women were in administrative and clerical positions though this covers a range of jobs from the senior to the lowly. In Nottingham City Council, 88 per cent of white women were below scale 4 on the APT&C grades while all black women were in these lower grade posts. There is little evidence for the professions, though work done by the NFHA (1987: 6) may serve as an indicator:

housing associations working in inner city areas house a significant number of black employees but they tend not to employ them.

In London 11.5 per cent of association employees were black while the rest of the country could only point to 4.5 per cent. Unfortunately this survey did not explore grade or type of job.

A further NFHA report (1989) states that black people are either absent or under represented in large sections of the work force and, once in, suffer as women do, from vertical segregation since they figure in the ranks of the lowest paid and occupy jobs considered less desirable. In most local authorities black women have 'no presence' in the managerial level but are considerably over represented at the low grade manual end of operations (Coyle, 1989).

The Federation of Black Housing Organisations (FBHO) has revealed apathy to equal opportunities in relation to black people through its examination of job adverts placed in 'Housing Association Weekly'. (Black Housing, 1990). In the period examined there were 166 adverts from registered associations and of these 95 stated they were or were working toward being equal opportunities employers: 24 welcomed applications from under-represented minority groups while the 'remaining 71... either did not give equal opportunities a thought or, less probably, forgot to mention it'. The FBHO article found discrimination in some of the 71 adverts and highlighted the wording used by Jephson Homes H.A. that 'Preference will be given to members of the Institute of Housing' as largely ruling out black applicants. Obviously this is a matter of concern for professional bodies that they are viewed as having a 'white' image. For black people, entry to such professions may be seen as limited to those with certain educational achievements which may represent a system which they believe militates against them.

Disabled people

It is clear that the chances of someone with a disability being unemployed are significantly higher than someone without a disability. The 1989 E.C. Labour Force Survey puts the rate at 20.5% and 5.4% respectively (Department of Employment, 1990).

Not only is there greater likelihood of unemployment but the period of unemployment is likely to be longer than for an able bodied person. Looking at the figures for those disabled people in paid work, interesting patterns emerge about the relative position of men and women.

It is interesting to note, from the table opposite, that, whether disabled or not, men and women's employment patterns are the same with women only getting ahead of men in clerical and administrative posts and in the unskilled and semi skilled / personal services. Between able bodied and disabled men, the disabled man takes on the woman's place, as it were, with a poorer showing except in junior white collar posts and those at the bottom end of the socio economic ladder. Between disabled and able bodied women there are more marked differences with disabled women showing up more frequently in the three lowest categories. In the top positions, disabled and able bodied women have the same ranking indicating perhaps that gender is a more serious barrier than disability.

What Martin's table does not show is whether these workers were employed at this level prior to disability or whether they gained entry into a post after the onset of disability.

Socio-economic status of men and women under pension age according to sex and whether disabled or not (%).

Socio-economic group	Disabled		Non Disabled	
	M	F	M	F
Professional	3	1	8	1
Employer/managerial	15	6	20	8
Intermediate non manual	19	16	10	20
Junior non manual	10	28	8	34
Skilled manual and own account non professional	37	12	37	8
Semi skilled manual and personal service	19	26	14	23
Unskilled	7	11	4	6

(Source: Martin et al, 1989, Disabled Adults: Services, Transport and Employment, Table 7.20)

Patricia Prescott-Clarke's work (1990) suggested that those born with a disability were more likely to be without work than those who become disabled while working. From this it might be inferred that those in high status jobs may have become disabled while those in low grade jobs are probably those born with disabilities. Given the earlier examination of black people it is fair to suggest, though research is lacking, that to be black and disabled is to count oneself lucky in having any job!

Central government has instituted legal redress for women and for black men and women who determine that they have been discriminated against in the recruitment or promotion field. No great claims can be made for the Industrial Tribunal procedure, succinctly analysed by McCrudden, Smith and Brown (1991:278):

Given the amount of time and trouble involved, it is surprising that so many applicants persist. There is clear evidence that honour and self respect are at stake. A rational person would not embark on the process of making a complaint of racial discrimination to a tribunal purely for the prospect of a monetary compensation which amounts to an 18% chance of obtaining a sum of £500 or more after a procedure lasting six to twelve months.

While this is true, it is important to note that a disabled person whose application is dropped in the bin because they are disabled, has no redress at all. Government has tried to tackle the problems of unemployment for disabled people by introducing a number of initiatives:

• Employment Rehabilitation centres

• Adult Training centres

• Institutionally Secured employment

- Sheltered workshop

- Sheltered placement

- Registration and quota schemes.

The quota scheme will be discussed in some detail but the essence of the others is that they offer low paid work (sometimes no pay at all), generally see disabled people as only being employable in segregated sectors and offer little, if any, opportunity to join the mainstream workforce (Barnes, 1991: 62-97).

The Disabled Persons (Employment) Acts 1944 and 1958 established the 3 per cent quota (those who employ more than twenty people should ensure that 3 per cent of the workforce is registered disabled) which is mandatory on the private sector though local authorities are expected to accept the same level of responsibility.

By 1979 only 36 per cent of Welsh local authorities had met the quota while the figure was down to 23 per cent for the Scottish and 13 per cent for English authorities. It is common practice for employers to apply for a bulk permit issued by the Manpower Services Training Agency which enables them to ignore the quota with impunity. Figures for 1990 reveal a worsening position with the average employment of disabled persons amounting to around 1 per cent of the workforce.

	Meet quota	Average	No of disabled
Eng/Welsh District	5.19%	1.1%	8080
London Boroughs	3.03%	0.7%	1703
Scots Districts	9.43%	1.3%	797
Scots Island Councils	0	0.9%	46

(Employment Gazette, 1991)

Those who fail to apply for a permit and fail to fill their quota will not brought in line by the penalties: in the 36 years between 1944 and 1980 there have been only 10 prosecutions for non compliance and in seven cases fines were levied though the total amount for all cases was a derisory £334.

It is fair to point out that this does not present a complete picture of the employment of disabled people. Many employees will be disabled persons who are not registered. Registration, however, is seen by many as the reason why they don't get appointed or even shortlisted.

Many organisations have advocated abolition of the quota though disabled people do not. What is needed is more teeth to the legislation. In 1992 it seems reasonable to look to continental Europe for good models. France is heartening. There recent legislation means that an employer must allocate 6 per cent of posts to disabled workers or pay a lump sum to a fund intended to improve disabled persons job prospects. Those who fail to comply are fined in the form of a penalty for each worker not recruited plus a 25 per cent surcharge (Equal Opportunity Review, 1988).

Perhaps because of the different legal positions, issues of equal opportunities in employment seem to be largely about race and gender. Bernard Leach (1989), in his examination of the appointments pages of *The*

Guardian, found a higher level of overt declarations mentioning race and gender than those speaking of disability.

The older worker

The position of older workers is confused. On the one hand there is pressure for the older worker to leave, perhaps to save younger people from being made redundant, and on the other, there seem to be trends from large retailers that the lack of school leavers has led to more job opportunities for older people. The first can be seen as ageism: given that it is generally more difficult for an older person to get a job the logical step is to shed younger workers who have a better chance of making a fresh start. The latter looks like progress but that depends whether sitting at a check out or measuring up kitchens for new fitments is attractive.

Throughout the eighties there have been significant falls in activity rate for men until it is now estimated that in the five year period prior to official retirement only about 55 per cent of men are in employment (Trinder, 1991). While the position of women seems more stable, women are often to be found in low paid, part time posts without the redundancy packages that many men can look forward to. The timing of this slump in employment for older workers suggests that the economic recession has played a part. This is true both in the shedding of their labour and their poor chances of recovery: many older workers are in manufacturing industries or coal mining which have both suffered great decline since 1980. Trinder's work suggests that older workers are less enthusiastic about moving for jobs and retraining which will bring them time limited benefits at the cost of personal upheaval. The reluctance does not exist only on the employees side. A Department of Employment Survey in 1988 of individuals attending courses or receiving job-related training, found that just 4.5 per cent of economically active men aged 50-59 and 1.9 per cent of those aged 60-64 had received some form of course or training in the four weeks prior to the interview (Laczko and Phillipson, 1990). The kinds of jobs now on offer are often of a highly technological nature but Trinder (1991) rightly points out that this can be overstated as an impediment to training and employment. Many have children who use computers at home and having gained familiarity with new technology there is little hostility to it in the workplace. What then is the problem, is it that there is insufficient work to provide jobs for all and older workers are seen as having had their share of work? Given the demographic trends which is decreasing the pool of younger workers this seems to be based on assumptions about older workers rather than facts.

Barriers

Suitability or acceptability?

Richard Jenkins (1986), in his exploration of racial disadvantage, concludes that it is not that they are unsuitable (underqualified) but that it is considered that they will be judged unacceptable as colleagues or to members of the public who are customers. Conforming to (real or imagined) employee or customer preference on race or gender is unlawful but when accepted is a way of keeping black people and women 'in their place'.

This section examines the use of stereotyping and sex typing by employers to present women, black persons, older workers and disabled persons as unsuitable for certain tasks .

In spite of the progress made by women, the eleven year prime ministership of a woman is an obvious example, stereotypes about women still abound. David Collinson (1988 and 1990) gives many examples of sexist attitudes among employers and sex typing of jobs. Collinson cites the ways in which firms seek to rationalise their discrimination:

Its something we've thought about for a long time, and its not for anti feminist reasons. But just because, a woman, if we're looking for long term stability, she can get engaged, married, have a baby and you know...off (Collinson et al, 1990: 97).

Even where women stayed in employment they were viewed as unstable because they were too 'aggressive':

Over the years men generally have been very much more successful, more stable, and we're looking for stability (Collinson et al, 1990: 97).

The ideal recruit was plainly a man who had a non working wife and had the commitments of home, mortgage and children. As many commentators have said the taking on of commitments is a sign of responsibility for a man but for a woman is a signal that she will put her career second or third behind husband and children.

The Women and Work Training days undertaken by North Tyneside MBC's Housing Department (1986) reveal women talking of the old boys network and men's attitudes which militated against women. A survey of women's views conducted by *The Guardian* (1991) indicated that 55 per cent of women felt that men's attitudes had not changed in the last 21 years and 51 per cent of women managers felt discriminated against in the workplace.

Disabled people are often presented as needy victims who are dependent on others and essentially vulnerable. Little wonder that employers see disabled persons as liabilities rather than useful potential workers or managers.

The interview started off with the old line, this is an informal interview so we won't be going round, we'll just ask the questions as they come... (Holdsworth, quoted in Sutherland, 1990).

Compare this with the following extract revealing the experiences of a young black man. For both candidates the interview is a charade because both have already been judged 'not our kind of person' before they begin:

John, aged 20, has 8 O levels and 1 A level, and has had 18 months experience working as a clerical officer. He applied for a position with another company. When he arrived at the interview he recognised one of the other candidates, a White male, who had less experience and fewer qualifications than John. While the White candidate's interview lasted approximately 25 minutes, John's only lasted for 10 minutes, of which the majority was taken by irrelevant questioning. Several days later John got the rejection letter he had expected saying "sorry but due to the high standards of competition, etc. etc." John later learned that the white male candidate with his lesser experience and qualifications had got the job (Gifford et al, 1989: 138).

The Equal Opportunities Commission (1989) monitored 11,373 job adverts in a wide range of periodicals covering the full range of professions. They found that over 25 per cent stated an age preference which was generally for applicants under the age of 45 but worryingly 65 per cent of those setting an age limit specified applicants under 35. This practice does not only affect the 'top jobs', employers seeking receptionists or other 'meet the public' posts may be looking for a more glamorous (younger) woman. It is only a few years since air hostesses were given ground duties after the age of 35 presumably because they were judged to be 'long in the tooth'.

Role models

The lack of high ranking black people and disabled people serves to flash a warning to these groups that this level of work is not suited to them. The North Tyneside Women in Housing group commented that women were often socialized into believing they could not be managerial material. This was often reinforced by a lack of women in senior management positions which reinforces the notion that these positions are jobs only for the boys. Legge (1978), talking of this in relation to women, cautions against putting too much faith in the solitary senior woman saying:

If some women succeed, the illusion of equal opportunities is maintained as the unsuccessful may be portrayed as inadequate rather than discriminated against.

Coyle goes further by suggesting that such women:

... find that they are highly visible and their professionalism undermined. They are perceived as having been appointed not because of their competence and expertise but because of an E.O. policy which "discriminates" against white males (Coyle, 1989: 46).

Informal relationships

Most of us have worked in organisations in which major decisions have been made not in the office but in the pub afterwards (Sandercock and Forsyth, 1990). Women may find themselves deliberately excluded by male colleagues or excluded because of a lack of women to go with or fear that a lone woman among men will be seen with a sexual gloss. The need to take part in these important informal networks may subject a woman to great pressure: consider how such networks militate against those from different religious and cultural backgrounds when taboos prevent socialising with men or alcohol. Consider the everyday access problems faced by the disabled whose social lives are confined by steps and narrow doorways.

It is assumed that women are unable to make a full commitment to their career. Angela Coyle (1989: 42) makes an important point:

> expectations of career patterns in local government actually conform to male patterns, so that at an age when most men are consolidating their careers most women will be having children. This means that if women are to keep apace with their male counterparts they have some rather insidious choices to make whether to have children or not; whether to spend time with their children during their early infancy; or whether to return to work as soon as possible after childbirth in order to retain at least a tenuous hold on future career development prospects.

The ROOF article on women directors of housing highlighted that all were childless and many were divorced.

Solutions

There are a number of approaches to the challenge of creating and sustaining a workforce which reflects the communities served. The first of these is the regulation of practice and the second is positive action.

Regulation

Any organisation seeking to institute an equal opportunities policy must follow these steps:

• Examine the employment profile with particular reference to the number of women, of disabled persons, of black men and women. What sections do they work in and what is their salary level?

• Examine job applicants. How many applications are there for each post and who are they. Was the advert external or internal or both. How many of those applicants from under-represented groups were short listed or offered posts?

• Examine the organisation section by section. Is there a sex balance? Are there black men and women working there and are any workers disabled? Is there discrimination or is it that applicants come from only one sex and/or racial group and are all able bodied? What can be done to achieve a better balance?

• Produce a statement backed with a policy, targets, strategies, monitoring procedures and feedback of results. This should involve training for staff, particularly those involved in recruitment and promotion.

Many employers while stressing that they have an equal opportunities statement plainly have only that. NFHA found that only 15 per cent of their respondents kept ethnic records of staff and only 22 per cent did so for job applicants. Without such records no employer can be certain that their policy statement is a statement of truth. The natural progression from such a base is the formalizing of recruitment which involves producing job descriptions and person specifications which are drawn up with a critical awareness of how easy it is to discriminate against certain groups by including unnecessary elements. The most common is tacking on the requirement for a driving license or even car ownership which discriminates the blind and also against many women who are less likely to be drivers and even less likely to be car owners than men.

Positive action

Those actively seeking to change their employee profile can do much to make a faster impact:

• Identify jobs where an employee of a particular racial group is needed. Under both Race Relations and Sex Discrimination legislation provision is made for positive action to meet the needs of one sex and or racial group.

• Using the wording to give specific encouragement to members of minority ethnic groups or disabled persons.

• Advertise in different places for example the ethnic minority press or use community groups as a recruiting source. They could reach different segments of the community.

• Allocate responsibility for recruitment of under-represented groups to a specific personnel officer.

The example of Lambeth demonstrates what could be done given political will. In Lambeth in May 1986, the Council decided not to apply for its block exemption from the 3 per cent quota. Having taken this step they had until the end of May to meet the quota which in effect meant that Lambeth could only appoint disabled people to any vacant post. This policy was in force till the end of August 1986 and by that time Lambeth had almost achieved its 3 per cent target from its base position of 0.9 per cent. Lambeth used advertising to target the disabled as well as open days for disabled people and a policy that any disabled person meeting the paper qualifications would be guaranteed an interview. Far from taking on employees purely because they were disabled, many talented people were taken from the local community who would have been taken up by other employers had they been able bodied. Lambeth also threw their posts open to the disabled whether registered or not with the proviso that those appointed should become registered in order to assist Lambeth with its quota target (Leach, 1989).

Supply side issues

As Collinson rightly asserts the process of regulation on its own will not totally remove discrimination since regulatory policies regarding recruitment and selection only deal with labour demand factors while the primary supply side constraint is the:

less than proportionate possession of those attributes which employers will take to constitute "employability" (Young, 1987: 104).

Chief among these for black applicants are the lack of formal qualifications and work experience. These, of course, are circular arguments for until black people:

can break through into secure and high status employment they will continue to be excluded from it on just grounds (Young, 1988: 105).

Since 1984 eight projects have been set up in different parts of the country specifically to train black people with housing associations and local authorities. *Black Housing* reporting on the West Midlands scheme found that, of the nine successful trainees from 1988/89, three obtained jobs with Birmingham City Council as Resettlement Officer, Housing Benefit Officer and Housing Assistant. One trainee secured a Housing Officer's post with Newham Council, and the remaining five secured jobs with various housing associations in Birmingham and Coventry.

Another example of good practice is illustrated by the private sector's Windsor Fellowships.

This scheme identifies black and Asian students intending to go into higher education and matches them with companies offering suitable career opportunities. These fellows are expected to act as role models for younger students and support each other. Fellows are not guaranteed jobs nor are they obliged to take up posts but all employers interviewed stated that they would want their fellows to work for their company (Employment Gazette, 1988).

For most women the battle to enter the workforce has been waged and won, the battle is now to pass the glass ceiling. This is not simply a matter of qualification it is a matter of confidence and feeling that a management presence from women would be welcome. North Tyneside MBC Housing Department held a series of women's training days which developed this agenda of positive action for women employees:

• Developmental and confidence building courses for women.

• A women's newsletter to bring women in the organisation together.

• There should be annual appraisal in which women could talk in confidence about their career paths and how to bridge their training gaps.

• There should be an annual women's day to promote the image of women and act as a support for women.

• Regular meetings of a women's group.

• Training for men on women's issues.

• Transport organised for women attending day release courses at a distance.

• Provide training to meet the special needs of employees or assisting with community schemes for this purpose.

• Provide training for those not employed.

Maggie Lancelot's study (1990) of women social workers in Bradford revealed that 31 per cent thought the male model of management was off putting. 23 per cent felt that to be a manager would mean conforming to a male management ethos because there was no alternative agenda or system of values. This creeping hard managerialism (Coyle 1989) has become a strong feature of the 80s and 90s. The 9 to 5 day has been superseded by the 5am to 9pm day. This is not a regime which is conducive either to individual health and happiness or indeed long term increases in productivity. More employers are recognising the problems caused by stress. Perhaps we need a different approach:

> As more women move higher up the organisation the greater the potential for a management model based in the utilisation of human resources... the recognition and value of co-operative ways of working as well as the need to work within constraints and be accountable to the public as users and politicians. Management could then concentrate on empowering the personal resources of the workers to deliver the service, with a less hierarchical structure which allows for dialogue rather than dissemination (Lancelot, 1990: 22).

Child care

For many women a career is combined with child care. British child care provision is very poor as the following comparison with Denmark indicates

---

U.K.
1% of under 5's are in local authority day nurseries which are not generally available to the average employed parent. 23% of children are in part time nurseries which allows women the opportunity to work part time. 40% of 3-4 year olds are in school because of early start to formal education but none have organised out of school hours care.

DENMARK
44% of under 3's / 80% of 3-7 year olds and 20% of 7-10 year olds have after school care places. Denmark spends six times as much as Britain (as expressed in % of GNP) and consequently only 10% of mothers do not work. All child care is publicly funded.

British employers both public and private sector, pay scant attention to family requirements and without good childcare facilities carers will simply suffer from 'exhaustion and psychological stress' (Nevill, Pennicott, Williams and Worrall, 1990: 41). Collinson goes further in stating:

More than any other measure, the socialisation of child care would establish the conditions whereby good equal opportunity practices could be taken for granted as the "normal" the "natural". For against this background, recruiters, job seekers and employees could be treated and treat themselves primarily as human beings who may be parents rather than primarily as men and women who will inevitably conform to the stereotype identities of bread winner and home maker. The introduction of creche facilities for the children of male and female employees is a crucial factor in undermining the defensive retreat into conventional gender identities which reflects and reinforces organisational power inequalities (Collinson, 1990: 211).

Perhaps employers will only start to take up these issues when the rising divorce/single parent tide and the growth in the dependent elderly begins to impact upon men. However the measures that could be taken are not new or untried.

• Job retainer schemes

• Placement schemes

• Refresher training schemes

• Job share

• 9 day fortnight

• Flexi time

• Flexible hours

• Parental leave

• Work place nurseries.

Taxation of work place child care is often raised as a barrier, however Nevill et al (1990) gives an example of the Kingsway Childrens Centre which is shared between six organisations in London. Charges are about £105 per week per child but the employer contributes 2/3, leaving parents to pay about £35 per week. The addition of tax means the cost per child is about £50 for parent/s.

What is needed is not an increase in new strategies but a new way of thinking about employment and workers. At present the number of hours worked and the importance of a post are too tightly bound up together and individuals with care responsibilities may feel that to suggest change is to be seen as having a lesser commitment to the job.

Conclusions

It is easy to become cynical and despondent about equal opportunities issues in the field of employment. Numerous good practice guides have been issued and yet progress on the whole has been slow and there is still a bed-rock of resistance to making change. For real change, there is a need to do more than adopt new regulatory procedures. Yes, these will help and will open up organisations and new markets for employers and employees but positive action leading to a more fundamental change of culture is necessary for all workers to be seen as workers first and not viewed on the basis of gender, race or disability or age.

References

Collett, S. & Ogden, G. & Hesmondhaugh, J. (1989), "Women, Planning and Equality", Department of Town and Country Planning, University of Newcastle upon Tyne.

Collinson, D. (1988), *Barriers to Fair Selection*, Equal Opportunities Commission, HMSO, London.

Collinson, D. & Knights, D. & Collinson, M. (1990), *Managing to Discriminate*, RKP, London.

Coyle, A. (1989), "The Limits of Change in Local Government and Equal Opportunities for Women", *Public Administration*, Vol 67, Spring: 39-50.

Department of Employment (1990), *Employment and Training for People with Disabilities: Consultative Document,* Department of Employment, London.

Employment Gazette (1991), "Registered Disabled People in the Public Sector", February: 79-83.

Employment Gazette (1988), "First Steps to the Top", January.

Equal Opportunities Review (1988), "French Disablement Initiative", No 17, Jan/Feb: 5.

Freathy, P. (1991), "Black workers and the YTS: A Case of Discrimination", *Critical Social Policy*, Issue 32, Autumn: 82-97.

Jenkins, R. (1986), *Racism and Recruitment: managers, organisations and equal opportunities in the labour market*, Cambridge University Press, Cambridge.

Julienne, L. (1990), "Monitoring H.A.s on Race Equality Issues", *Black Housing*, Nov/Dec: 4-8.

Gifford, T. & Brown, W. & Bundey, R. (1988), *Loosen The Shackles*, Keria Press, London.

Greed, C. (1990), "The Professional and the Personal" in Stanley, L. (ed), *Feminist Praxis*, Routledge, London.

Institute of Housing (1986), *The Key to Inequality*, IoH, London.

Laczko, F. & Phillipson, C. (1990), "Defending the Right to Work", in (ed), McEwen, E. *Age: The Unrecognised Discrimination*, Age Concern, London,

Lancelot, M. (1990), "A Fitting Model for the 90s", *Community Care*, July 5th.

Leach, B. (1989), "Disabled People and the Implementation of Local Authorities' Equal Opportunities Policies", *Public Administration*, Vol 67, Spring: 65-77.

Lewis, S. (1991), "Breaking through the glass ceiling", *The Journal of the American Planning Association*, July: 7-13.

Local Government Training Board (1990), *The Disabling Council*, (video).

McCrudden, C.; Smith, D. J. & Brown, C. (1991), *Racial Justice at Work*, PSI, London.

Mihill, C. (1991), "Surgical Sexism barrier to women consultants", *The Guardian*, January 23rd: 8.

National Federation of Housing Associations (1985), *Women in Housing: Employment*.

NFHA (1987), *Race... Still A Cause for Concern*.

NFHA (1989), *Race and Housing: Employment and Training Guide*.

Nevill, G. & Pennicott, A. & Willliams, J. & Worrall, A. (1990), *Women in the Workforce: The Effects of Demographic Changes in the 1990s*, Industrial Society, London.

North Tyneside MBC (1986), "Women, Work and Training".

Ohri, S. & Faruqi, S. (1988), in Bhat, A. Carr-Hill, R. & Ohri, S.(eds), *Britain's Black Population*, Gower, Aldershot.

Oliver, M. (1990), *The Politics of Disablement*, Macmillan, London.

Prescott-Clarke, P. (1990), *Employment and Handicap*, SCPR, London.

ROOF (1990), "New Operators on the old Boys Network", Nov/Dec: 22-25

Sandercock, L. & Forsyth, A. (1990), " Gender: A New Agenda for Planning Theory", Working Paper 521, University of Berkeley at California.

Sheffield City Council (1989), "Guide-lines on Disadvantaged Groups and their Needs: Client Sub-group."

Stone, I. (1988), *Equal Opportunities in Local Authorities*, Equal Opportunities Commission Research Series, HMSO, London.

Sutherland, A. (1990), *The Disabling Council*, Local Government Training Board, Luton.

Townsend,P. (1989), "Employment and Disability" in Walker, A. & Townsend, P. (eds), *Disability in Britain: A Manifesto of Rights*, Martin Robertson and Co. Ltd, London.

Trinder, C. (1991), "How much employment after 55?," *Findings*, Joseph Rowntree Memorial Trust, York.

University of Newcastle upon Tyne (1992),"Newcastle's West End. Monitoring the City Challenge Initiative: A Baseline Report", Newcastle upon Tyne.

Young, K. (1987), "The Space Between Words", in Jenkins, R. and Solomos, J.(eds), *Racism and Equal Opportunities policies in the 1980s*, Cambridge University Press, Cambridge.